D0823337

DUBLIN
ENCOUNTER

FIONN DAVENPORT

Dublin Encounter

Published by Lonely Planet Publications Pty Ltd
ABN 36 005 607 983

Australia (Head Office)	Locked Bag 1, Footscray, Vic 3011 ☎ 03 8379 8000 fax 03 8379 8111 talk2us@lonelyplanet.com.au
USA	150 Linden St, Oakland, CA 94607 ☎ 510 250 6400 toll free 800 275 8555 fax 510 893 8572 info@lonelyplanet.com
UK	2nd fl, 186 City Rd London EC1V 2NT ☎ 020 7106 2100 fax 020 7106 2101 go@lonelyplanet.co.uk

This title was commissioned in Lonely Planet's London office and produced by: **Commissioning Editors** Clifton Wilkinson, Emma Gilmour **Coordinating Editor** Saralinda Turner **Coordinating Cartographer** Jacqueline Nguyen **Layout Designer** Margaret Jung **Assisting Editor** Paul Harding **Managing Editor** Bruce Evans **Managing Cartographers** David Connolly, Herman So **Cover** Image Research provided by lonelyplanetimages.com **Project Manager** Eoin Dunlevy **Managing Layout Designer** Laura Jane **Thanks to** Lucy Birchley, Melanie Dankel, Sally Darmody, Katie Lynch, Trent Paton, Simon Tillema, Brian Turnbull

ISBN 978 1 74179 146 4

Printed through Colorcraft Ltd, Hong Kong. Printed in China.

Acknowledgement Dublin Transit Map © 2006 – 2009 Irish Rail

Mixed Sources
Product group from well-managed forests and other controlled sources
www.fsc.org Cert no. SGS-COC-005002
© 1996 Forest Stewardship Council

HOW TO USE THIS BOOK
Colour-Coding & Maps
Colour-coding is used for symbols on maps and in the text that they relate to (eg all eating venues on the maps and in the text are given a green knife and fork symbol). Each neighbourhood also gets its own colour, and this is used down the edge of the page and throughout that neighbourhood section.

Prices
Multiple prices listed with reviews (eg €10/5 or €10/5/20) indicate adult/child, adult/concession or adult/child/family.

Send us your feedback We love to hear from readers – your comments help make our books better. We read every word you send us, and we always guarantee that your feedback goes straight to the appropriate authors. The most useful submissions are rewarded with a free book. To send us your updates and find out about Lonely Planet events, newsletters and travel news visit our award-winning website: **lonelyplanet.com/contact**.

Note: We may edit, reproduce and incorporate your comments in Lonely Planet products such as guidebooks, websites and digital products, so let us know if you don't want your comments reproduced or your name acknowledged. For a copy of our privacy policy visit **lonelyplanet.com/privacy**.

FIONN DAVENPORT

Half Italian and a lifelong supporter of Liverpool Football Club, Fionn is the perfect Dubliner, in love with the city of his birth but one eye forever on somewhere else. He's left his city many times – for years at a stretch – but always he returns, because it's the only place on earth that treats gallows humour as high art; why look for a straight answer when a funny one is far more satisfying?

FIONN THANKS

My thanks to Saralinda Turner and Clifton Wilkinson for understanding the concept of elastic time; and to Caroline Clarke for everything else.

Our readers Many thanks to the travellers who wrote to us with helpful hints, useful advice and interesting anecdotes. Katie Bale, Jose Kawas, Keith Kenney, Johanna King, Marieke Koets, Outi Kyyts, Ruth McDermott, James Moran, Sven Naumann, Chris Nivard, Kate O'Reilly, Sally St Clair, Harvey and Valerie Turer.

Cover photograph Strolling across the Liffey, Dublin, NUTAN/APHO. **Internal photographs** p76, p89, p101 by Fionn Davenport; p19 B O'Kane/Alamy. All other photographs by Lonely Planet Images, and by Doug McKinlay except p24 Conor Caffrey; p123 Sean Caffrey; p6 (left and right), p30 (bottom), p42, p45, p55, p61, p125, p141 Olivier Cirendini; p23 Ian Connellan; p28, p32, p34, p77, p106, p112 Richard Cummins; p21 Wade Eakle; p29, p30 (left) John Elk III; p128 Rick Gerharter; p6 (bottom) Corinne Humphrey; p74 Holger Leue; p12, p20, p41, p132 Hannah Levy; p146 Gareth McCormack; p72, p129 Martin Moos; p48, p59 Stephen Saks; p14, p16, p17, p46, p70, p79, p85, p99, p113, p124, p138, p145, p151 Jonathan Smith; p8 John Sones; p10, p111, p143 Oliver Strewe; p4, p25 Wayne Walton; p102 Corey Wise.

All images are copyright of the photographers unless otherwise indicated. Many of the images in this guide are available for licensing from **Lonely Planet Images:** lonelyplanetimages.com

Bringing portraiture to the masses in Grafton St (p38)

CONTENTS

THE AUTHOR	**03**	**> MUSIC**	**148**	
THIS IS DUBLIN	**07**	**> SHOPPING**	**149**	
HIGHLIGHTS	**08**	**> THEATRE**	**150**	
DUBLIN DIARY	**23**	**BACKGROUND**	**151**	
ITINERARIES	**29**	**DIRECTORY**	**158**	
NEIGHBOURHOODS	**34**	**INDEX**	**170**	

>GRAFTON STREET &
  AROUND   38
>GEORGIAN DUBLIN   52
>TEMPLE BAR   64
>SODA   78
>KILMAINHAM &
  THE LIBERTIES   96
>O'CONNELL STREET &
  AROUND   104
>SMITHFIELD &
  PHOENIX PARK   120
>BEYOND THE
  GRAND CANAL   126

SNAPSHOTS   **134**
> ACCOMMODATION   136
> DRINKING   138
> KIDS   140
> ARCHITECTURE   141
> CLUBBING   142
> FOOD   143
> GAELIC FOOTBALL   144
> GARDENS & PARKS   145
> GAY & LESBIAN   146
> JAMES JOYCE   147

Why is our travel information the best in the world? It's simple: our authors are passionate, dedicated travellers. They don't take freebies in exchange for positive coverage so you can be sure the advice you're given is impartial. They travel widely to all the popular spots, and off the beaten track. They don't research using just the internet or phone. They discover new places not included in any other guidebook. They personally visit thousands of hotels, restaurants, palaces, trails, galleries, temples and more. They speak with dozens of locals every day to make sure you get the kind of insider knowledge only a local could tell you. They take pride in getting all the details right, and in telling it how it is. Think you can do it? Find out how at **lonelyplanet.com**.

THIS IS DUBLIN

Definition of a top class city: a place that makes virtue out of vice, knows exactly where to find fun, and doesn't worry about getting any sleep. Welcome to Dublin, contender for greatest European city.

Dubs can be brutally unsentimental about their city, which mightn't come across as quite so sexy or sultry as other European capitals, but Dublin, they'll tell you, has *personality*, which is way more important than good looks and will last far longer.

So, what is it that makes Dublin so special?

One, it's small. The city centre is bordered by two canals, north and south, and you can get anywhere on foot (or, as Dubliners might say, at least anywhere that's worth going). Two, it's lively. With one of the youngest populations of any city in Europe, Dublin is alive with bars, restaurants and nightlife and full of people who know how to live it large. Three, it's friendly. Lift a map to waist-level and you'll attract a host of locals who'll show you where to go and will probably walk part of the way with you. Four, it's cosmopolitan. Gone are the days when avocados were considered exotic and olive oil was only available from chemists. With a healthy and sizeable influx of foreign nationals over the last decade, Dublin has become a proper multicultural hub, something that has given the city's arts and culinary scene a good kick in the pants.

Oh yes, and there's the sights – although you'll be having such a good time you might not get to experience the wonders of the city's many museums and galleries, or take in the diverse architecture of its elegant Georgian squares and modernist docklands.

Dublin oozes character: it is a city whose sociability and soul will stay with you long after you travel home, and will guarantee that you'll soon be booking tickets for your return.

Top left Just me and my guitar – street musician in Temple Bar **Top right** Peacock fanlights, elegant columns and coloured doors epitomise Georgian Dublin **Bottom** Ornate iconography in the *Book of Kells* housed at Trinity College (p40)

>HIGHLIGHTS

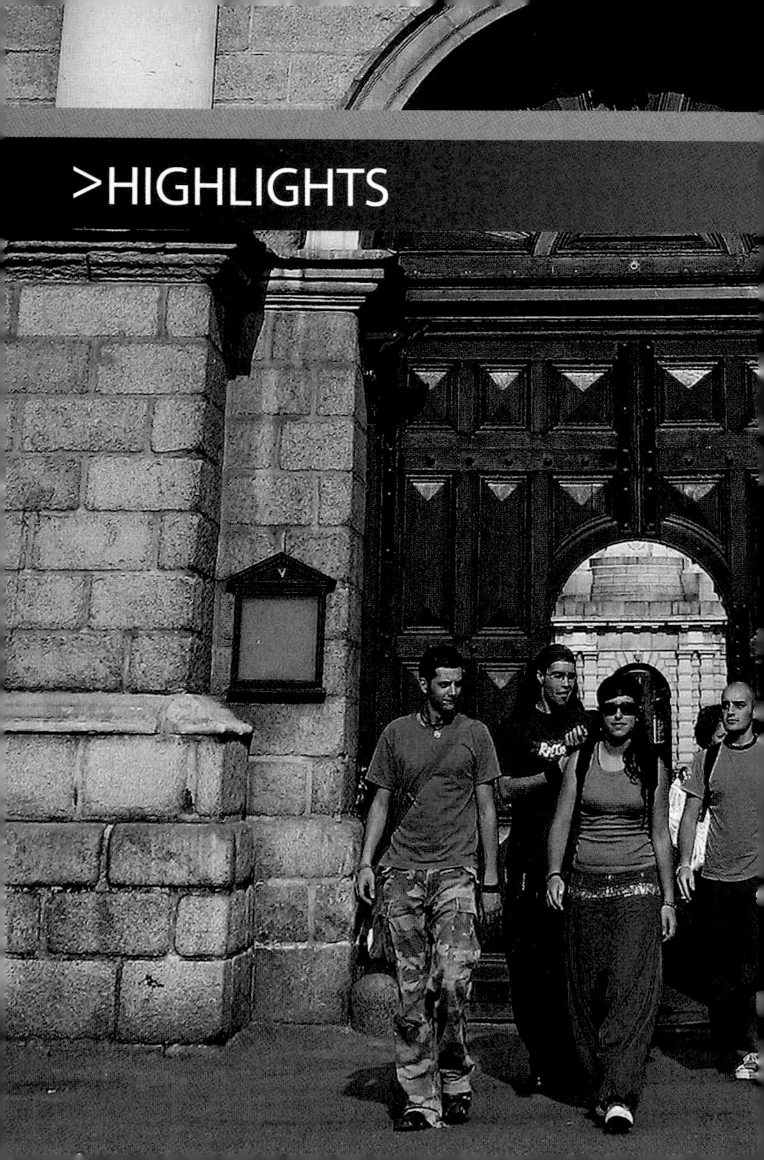

>1 Stroll through the lofty Elizabethan academe
of Trinity   10
>2 Sip a pint of black gold at the mother of all
breweries   12
>3 Play, stroll or snooze in Dublin's favourite
green lung   14
>4 Get in touch with your spiritual side   16
>5 Distinguish your Hirst from your Hockney in an
old soldiers' home   17
>6 Visit the gaol where beats the gruesome,
defiant heart of Irish history   18
>7 Enjoy food, beer and a damn good play   19
>8 Wet your lips by the hearth of Dublin's social
heart   20
>9 Lose your money and your voice in support of
sporting vice   21
>10 Bust an Irish move on the dance floor to impress
your friends   22

Just another day amid the Elizabethan splendour for students at Trinity College (p10)

>1 TRINITY COLLEGE

STROLL THROUGH THE LOFTY ELIZABETHAN ACADEME OF TRINITY

Entering through the Regent House archway onto Front Sq and leaving the noisy bustle of Dame St behind feels like you're stepping back in time to a more genteel era of august academia, cricket matches and Pimms parties on the lawn. There may be a debate over whether it's the city's foremost university, but there's no argument that it's by far the prettiest, the most central, and easily the most evocative of Dublin's institutes of higher learning (see p40 for more information).

It's been more than 400 years in the practice, ever since Elizabeth I granted a charter to its founders in 1592 so that they could stop Irish

THE CLONING OF THE LONG ROOM

The Long Room (pictured above) has a few screen credits to its name (*Educating Rita* for instance), but its unlikeliest appearance was in *Star Wars Episode II: Attack of the Clones*, when it showed up in CGI form as the Jedi Archive, complete with the same barrel-vaulted ceiling and similar statuary down its length. If nothing else, it makes for a good trivia question.

youth from being 'infected with popery'. (One of its early students, by the way, was Archbishop James Ussher, who dated the act of Creation to 4004 BC – we thought you'd want to know.) Today the bigotry that led to its establishment has been consigned to history, but there's no escaping the scent of privilege that pervades the place, from the cobbled squares lined with handsome Victorian buildings (although most of the original structures have long since been replaced) to the carefully manicured playing fields at the back, where on summer days cricket matches are played before an appreciative audience sitting on the deck of the Pavilion Bar, drinks in hand.

Dublin's very own slice of Oxbridge aside, Trinity is home to that most Irish of treasures, the *Book of Kells*, which ironically is not Irish at all but Scottish – for it was created on the island of Iona before being transported to Kells in AD 806 so that it wouldn't fall into the hands of Viking raiders. A glimpse of it is an absolute must, but it's about as much as you'll get – its popularity and the way it is exhibited ensures that visitors are ushered past quickly and efficiently, without any time to linger and savour its beauty.

>2 GUINNESS STOREHOUSE

SIP A PINT OF BLACK GOLD AT THE MOTHER OF ALL BREWERIES

More Dublin than Joyce, the Liffey and Temple Bar put together, Guinness is the very lifeblood of the city, the liquid that courses through the arteries of its streets, fuelling 1001 experiences daily. So what better place to sample a pint of the black gold than its spiritual home, where every year 450 million litres of the stuff is brewed and exported to 150 countries around the world?

G-FORCE GUINNESS

It might be an enduring favourite, but that isn't to say that Dublin's prized pint has remained unchanged since it first bubbled into existence in 1759. Ireland's new 9000-strong Nigerian community were dismayed to taste the 'watery' 4.5% alcohol brew on sale, which they felt paled in comparison to the potent 7.5% version back home. Nigeria is Guinness' third-largest market (after Ireland and Britain), and the increased volume harks back to the 18th century when fortified beer was produced to survive the ship's long journey to Africa. Guinness duly responded to the complaint, and now the famous Dublin Guinness Foreign Extra satisfies the discerning Nigerian palate.

Housed in an old grain storehouse opposite the original St James's Gate Brewery, this is the city's most visited tourist attraction, an all-singing, all-dancing extravaganza combining sophisticated exhibits, spectacular design and a thick, creamy head of marketing hype.

OK, so you'll make your way through the impressive building past the various exhibits outlining the history of the beer and the brewery, from the original charter (exhibited beneath the glass floor in the lobby) to a whole section devoted to advertising (the iconic poster and TV campaigns that have helped sell the brand world-wide). Some of the exhibits are indeed pretty fascinating, but who are we kidding? Your final destination is what this place is really all about – the top floor Gravity Bar, where you get to drink a free glass of Guinness with a 360-degree backdrop of the city. Guinness doesn't travel well, or so everyone believes, so the one you'll have here is reputedly the best one you'll have anywhere; hundreds of thousands of personalised tests, including our own, seem to validate the theory. It's cold, beautifully bitter and oh-so-very black, but the key ingredient to enjoying a pint is the company of friends, so make sure you have a couple of them around when you quaff that brew.

For more on the Guinness Storehouse see p99.

>3 ST STEPHEN'S GREEN

PLAY, STROLL OR SNOOZE IN DUBLIN'S FAVOURITE GREEN LUNG

Once upon a time, handsome St Stephen's Green was a common where public whippings, burnings and hangings took place; these days, the worst punishment is a telling off by the warden for careless cycling or for kicking a ball on the grass – with lawns like these, it's almost impossible to resist.

Workers at lunch, lovers and layabouts can be found splayed about its nine manicured hectares at the merest hint of sun, content

NO SUCH THING AS A FREE MUNCH

Dubliners U2 were conferred with Freedom of the City in a dazzling ceremony in 2000. Not shy of the odd publicity stroke, it didn't take Bono and the Edge long to invoke one of the ancient privileges of their new-found 'freedom' – the right to graze sheep on common ground within the city boundaries. It was an honour they duly carried out on the lawns of St Stephen's Green, to much public amusement, with two borrowed lambs the following morning.

among the green lawns and fowl-filled ponds, sharing food and a laugh with each other while the day is warm.

The fine Georgian buildings around the square date mainly from Dublin's 18th-century boom. During the 1916 Easter Rising, a band of Irish rebel forces occupied St Stephen's Green, led by the colourful Irish nationalist Countess Constance Markievicz, later the first woman elected to the Irish Parliament. Markievicz failed to take the grand Shelbourne Hotel, a popular society meeting place (although gunshots apparently disturbed the ladies at lunch, with bullets flying through the windows), but the rebels did seize the Royal College of Surgeons building on the western side of the square. If you look closely at its columns you can still see the bullet marks.

A few doors from the Shelbourne is a small Huguenot cemetery, established in 1693 for French Protestant refugees. The south side is home to the beautifully restored Newman House (p57) and the Byzantine-inspired Newman University Church (p57).

Statues and memorials dot the green, including those of Sir Arthur Guinness and James Joyce. Around the central fountain are busts of Countess Markievicz and a 1967 Henry Moore sculpture of WB Yeats.

Also see p58.

>4 CHESTER BEATTY LIBRARY

GET IN TOUCH WITH YOUR SPIRITUAL SIDE

Beyond the hubbub and ordinary distractions of the street lies one of Europe's most outstanding museums, a tranquil place of beauty and reflection whose astounding collection has the power to bring serenity and peace to all who visit. And the best bit is that relatively few people ever do!

The collection in question was gathered by New York mining magnate Sir Alfred Chester Beatty (1875–1968), whose passion for the intricately decorated manuscripts, bindings and calligraphies he found on his journeys to Egypt and the Far East resulted in his amassing more than 20,000 texts, scrolls, religious books and objets d'art, many of which are carefully displayed over two floors.

Unlike so many other museums, which seek to wow the visitor with scale, the Chester Beatty collection is compact and can be easily visited in no more than half an hour. But the muted ambience encourages you to slow down and savour each individual piece – or watch one of the many audiovisual displays explaining some feature or another.

Exquisite exhibits range from intricately designed medicine boxes and Chinese jade books, to ancient Egyptian papyri and an extraordinary collection of Korans (the best in the West).

When you're finally done with the collection, you can ponder the passage of life in the small Japanese Garden upstairs, or grab a tasty lunch in the Silk Road Cafe.

For further details see p79.

>5 IRISH MUSEUM OF MODERN ART (IMMA)

DISTINGUISH YOUR HIRST FROM YOUR HOCKNEY IN AN OLD SOLDIERS' HOME

Even if the thought of modern art leaves you cold, the setting of the IMMA will undoubtedly provide reason enough to visit. The country's top contemporary art gallery is spectacularly located in the former Royal Hospital Kilmainham, the city's finest surviving 17th-century building. The grounds, with their long tree-lined avenue and fountain-filled Formal Garden with views across the Liffey to Phoenix Park, make a fantastic place to stroll.

Built between 1680 and 1684, this fine building with a striking facade inspired by Les Invalides in Paris, is laid out with a central cobbled courtyard. Inside, the light-filled museum juxtaposes the work of major established artists with that of up-and-comers. The gallery's 4000-strong collection includes works by Picasso, Miró and Vasarely, as well as more contemporary artists including Gilbert and George, Gillian Wearing and Damien Hirst. The gallery displays ever-changing shows from its own collection, and also hosts touring exhibitions.

Modern Irish art is always on display and Irish and international artists live and work onsite in the converted coach houses. The New Galleries, in the restored Deputy Master's House, should not be missed.

For more on the museum see p99.

>6 KILMAINHAM GAOL

VISIT THE GAOL WHERE BEATS THE GRUESOME, DEFIANT HEART OF IRISH HISTORY

If you have any interest in Irish history, especially the juicy bits about resistance to English rule, you will be shaken and stirred by a visit to this infamous, eerie prison. It was the stage for many of the most tragic and heroic episodes in Ireland's recent past, and the list of its inmates reads like a who's who of Irish nationalism. Solid and sombre, its walls absorbed the tragic events under British occupation and recount it in whispers to every visitor.

After the 1916 Easter Rising, 14 of the 15 rebel executions took place at Kilmainham. James Connolly, who was so badly injured during fighting he couldn't stand, was strapped to a chair in the Execution Yard to face the firing squad. The ruthlessness of the killings outraged the public, both in Ireland and England, and boosted the nationalist cause.

The East Wing, modelled on London's Pentonville Prison, with metal catwalks suspended around a light-filled, vaulted room, allowed guards full view of all the cells. Graffiti, scratched and scrawled by prisoners in the cells, is moving stuff.

Guided tours to Kilmainham include an excellent museum, the prison chapel, the exercise and execution yards, and the dark, dank old wing. During the Great Famine, thousands of petty thieves, including children, were crammed in here.

See p100 for details.

>7 THE PLAY'S NOT THE ONLY THING

ENJOY FOOD, BEER AND A DAMN GOOD PLAY

Beckett, Synge, Shaw, Wilde…Dublin's not short of a theatrical genius or two, so a night at the theatre is absolutely necessary, daahling. But it'll take more than just the play, for any night out in Dublin has to involve food and booze somewhere along the way!

Start with the pretheatre special at Chapter One (p115), three tasty courses at one of Dublin's best restaurants, situated in the basement of the Dublin Writers Museum (p107). What's really special about this place is that they'll pick your theatre tickets up for you and deliver them to your table. Then, it's off to either Ireland's national theatre, the world-famous Abbey (p118), or the Gate (p118, pictured above) – where both James Mason and Orson Welles trod the boards in their youth – for the main event. When the curtain falls, make your way back to Chapter One for the remainder of your prandials, where you can dissect the merits of the show over dessert and coffee in the lounge or at the bar. To cap it off, make your way to one of the best traditional bars in town, the Sackville Lounge (p117), a favourite of thespians.

If you prefer to do your own ticketing, bookings can usually be made by credit card over the phone; you can collect your tickets just before the performance. Most plays begin at 8pm.

>8 VENERABLE DUBLIN INSTITUTIONS

WET YOUR LIPS BY THE HEARTH OF DUBLIN'S SOCIAL HEART

We're guessing you already know Dublin has its fair share of wonderful, atmospheric pubs – hey, it's probably what brought you here in the first place – but first-time visitors might be surprised by just how central the pub is to a Dubliner's social existence. The pub is a meeting point for friends and strangers alike, a place to mark a moment and pass the time, a forum for discourse and a temple of silent contemplation. It is where joy is toasted and sorrows drowned; for most it is where the night will end, but for some where the day begins: it is where Dubliners are at their friendly and convivial best – and at their drunken and belligerent worst.

There are pubs for every taste and sensibility, from no-fuss boozers like Mulligan's (p73) to raucous gay bars like Panti (p119), and every other kind in between, although the *truly* traditional haunts populated by flat-capped pensioners bursting with insightful anecdotes are, increasingly, as rare as hen's teeth. The magic, though, is far from dead, for it is not the spit or sawdust that makes a great Dublin pub, but the patrons themselves.

>9 GOING TO THE DOGS & OTHER SPORTING PURSUITS

LOSE YOUR MONEY AND YOUR VOICE IN SUPPORT OF SPORTING VICE

Dublin without sport is like…well, Guinness without the bishop's collar, so an afternoon or an evening in the company of Dubs pursuing their passion through bet and bellow is one of the best experiences you could ever have.

Gaelic sports – hurling and football – are a national religion, and Dublin is home to the high cathedral of both games. The best time to go to Croke Park (see p114, pictured above) is during the summer and early autumn, when the stadium becomes a cauldron of passion, especially if Dublin is playing in the Senior Football Championship. But the best of the Senior Hurling Championship is on here too, with the likes of Kilkenny, Cork and Tipperary displaying their consummate skills to packed houses in excess of 70,000.

You may think that the dog track (see p133) is the sole preserve of the gambling hound and other desperate types, but there's a surprise in store, especially if you don't fancy the idea of standing against the rail while the drizzle dampens the printed hopes you hold in your hand. No, you can experience the delight and dismay of a night at 'the dogs' from the comfort of a glass-enclosed stand, where your very own waiter-cum-bookie will bring you dinner and refreshments and process your bets right at the table.

HIGHLIGHTS

>10 YOUR OWN PERSONAL RIVERDANCE

BUST AN IRISH MOVE ON THE DANCE FLOOR TO IMPRESS YOUR FRIENDS

Irish dancing looks impossibly fast and complicated, especially if your only experience of it is the phenomenon that is Riverdance. Two little facts: the Riverdance kids are good, but it ain't all that traditional; and learning the basics is not nearly as difficult as you think.

The Comhaltas Ceoltóirí Éireann (p132, pictured above) – pronounced 'ko-ltass kee-oltory erin' and translated as the Organisation of Irish Musicians – is housed in the Cultúrlann na hÉireann (Irish Cultural Institute), the spiritual home of the traditional forms in Dublin, located in the southern suburb of Monkstown, which is easily reached from the city centre by DART. There are free, informal sessions of traditional music on Tuesday and Wednesday from 8pm; visitors are most welcome, and you can sit and tap your feet, get a bite to eat and have a few pints, all the while enjoying some of the best music around. But the real treat is on Friday night, where, for a nominal fee, you can participate in the *céilidh,* or group Irish dance, itself accompanied by live music. There are teachers on hand to help you with the basic steps, and if nothing else you can be guaranteed to learn how to stay on your feet during a jig, reel or square dance. It's an enormous amount of fun and one of the more memorable experiences of any trip to Dublin.

>DUBLIN DIARY

No matter what time of the year you're in town, there's always something on. No sooner does Christmas grind to a slow halt – sometime in January – than preparations begin for the mother of all piss-ups, ill-disguised as a celebration of Ireland's patron saint. Hardly a summer weekend goes by without there being some organised booty-shake or gourmet extravaganza. In between the big events, there are still a few quieter festivals to set your pulse racing.

Sporting shamrock spirit on St Patrick's Day (p24)

FEBRUARY

Jameson Dublin International Film Festival

☎ 872 1122; www.dubliniff.com

Local flicks, arty international films and advance screenings of mainstream movies make up the menu of the city's film festival.

Six Nations Championship

www.irishrugby.ie

The first rugby matches of the international calendar see Ireland pitted against England, Scotland, Wales, France and Italy. Matches are played at the Lansdowne Aviva Stadium (Map p127, E2).

MARCH

St Patrick's Festival

☎ 676 3205; www.stpatricksday.ie

The mother of all festivals. Hundreds of thousands gather to 'honour' St Patrick over four days around 17 March on city streets and in venues throughout the centre.

APRIL

Handel's Messiah

A performance is held outside what was once Neal's Music Hall, Fishamble St, in Temple Bar, to mark the occasion of the sacred piece's first performance on 13 April, 1742.

Performers channel magic and frivolity in Dublin's St Patrick's Day Parade

MAY

Mardi Gras

www.dublinpride.org

The last weekend of the month sees in Dublin's gay pride celebration, with a parade and other festivities.

Dublin Gay Theatre Festival

www.gaytheatre.ie

A fortnight devoted exclusively to gay theatre with plays by gay writers past and present that have a gay or gay-related theme.

JUNE

Convergence Festival

www.sustainable.ie

A 10-day green festival in Temple Bar focussed on renewable, sustainable living, with a diverse program of workshops, talks and children's activities.

Dublin Writers Festival

www.dublinwritersfestival.com

Four-day literature festival attracting Irish and international writers to its readings, performances and talks.

Diversions

☎ 677 2255; www.templebar.ie

Free outdoor music, and children's and film events on weekends from June to September in Temple Bar's Meeting House Sq (Map p65, C2).

Women's Mini Marathon

www.womensminimarathon.ie

A 10km charity run on the second Sunday of the month, attracting up to 40,000 participants — including some poorly disguised men — that is the largest of its kind in the world.

JULY

Bloomsday

www.jamesjoyce.ie

Celebrate *Ulysses* on the 16th of July with readings, wanderings, grub and costumes.

Bloomsday reading at the Joyce Centre (p108)

DUBLIN DIARY

Oxegen

www.oxegen.ie

Massive music festival over the July weekend closest to the 12th that usually manages to pack a few dozen heavyweight acts across six stages into its four-day line-up.

Liffey Swim

☎ 833 2434

Five hundred lunatics take to the river and swim 2.5km from Rory O'More Bridge to the Custom House – one can't help but admire their steely will.

WHEN IN DUBLIN...

Even if you can't make it into town for one of the major fixed events, keep your eyes peeled and your ears pricked for other flexible dates on the Dublin calendar. The awesome **Temple Bar Trad Festival of Irish Music and Culture** (www.templebartrad.com) is a mouthful, but it's three days of quality music at the beginning of the year, with craft markets and workshops thrown in for good measure. **Tastefest** (www.rds.ie) is an actual mouthful of delicious gourmet delicacies that takes over the Royal Dublin Society around March. In June, look out for the **Street Performance World Championship** (www.spwc.ie) where the best pavement entertainers, from contortionists and comedians to magicians and musicians, go head-to-head in and around Merrion Sq (Map p53, D1).

AUGUST

Dublin Horse Show

www.rds.ie

The horsey set trot down to the capital for the social highlight of the year, climaxing in the Aga Khan Cup, an international-class competition.

Dun Laoghaire Festival of World Cultures

☎ 271 9555; www.festivalofworld cultures.com

Colourful multicultural music, art and theatre festival on the last weekend of the month.

SEPTEMBER

All-Ireland Finals

www.gaa.ie

Croke Park goes wild with the hurling finals (second Sunday of the month) and Gaelic football finals (fourth Sunday).

Dublin Fringe Festival

☎ 872 9016; www.fringefest.com

The 'alternative' theatre festival has in recent years earned as much critical kudos as the main festival.

Bulmers International Comedy Festival

www.bulmerscomedy.ie

Best of Irish and international comics wringing out the laughs.

The Olympia, one of Dublin's grand old stage dames, hosts performances during the Dublin Theatre Festival

OCTOBER

Dublin Theatre Festival

☎ 677 8439; www.dublintheatre festival.com

Europe's oldest theatre festival is a 2½-week showcase of Irish and international productions at various locations around town.

Hallowe'en

Tens of thousands take to the city streets for a night-time parade, fireworks, street theatre, music and drink to revel in this traditional pagan festival in celebration of the dead, the end of the harvest and the Celtic New Year.

NOVEMBER

French Film Festival

www.irishfilm.ie

Organised by the French embassy and sponsored by Carte Noir, this festival showcases the best of French releases for the year.

Junior Dublin Film Festival

www.ifi.ie

A weeklong showcase of the best efforts of the world's young filmmakers; the Irish Film Institute screens an exclusive selection of movies from all over.

A waxing gibbous moon rises above Sandycove's Martello tower

DECEMBER

Christmas Dip@the Forty Foot

Possibly the most hardcore hangover cure
known to man, this event takes place at 11am
on Christmas Day at the famous pool below
the Martello tower in Sandycove (p130).

Leopardstown Races

www.leopardstown.com

Historic and hugely popular racing festival at
one of Europe's loveliest courses – modelled
on Sandown Park Racecourse in England
and completed in 1888 – from 26 to 30
December.

>ITINERARIES

Kaleidoscopic bouquets for sale in the Grafton St mall

ITINERARIES

Taking in all of Dublin's highlights is a relatively straightforward task, made all the easier by the city's compact size, which keeps the schlepping to a manageable minimum. Still, with so much to see and do, you'll need some kind of a plan: you won't miss much if you follow the suggested itineraries here.

DAY ONE

Start early at Trinity College (p40) then ramble over to George's St Arcade (p84) to nose about the record and book stalls. For lunch, bag a hearty sandwich at Honest to Goodness (p88), then ramble up to the Guinness Storehouse (p99) for an hour or so. While you're in that neck of the woods, mosey around the Liberties (Map p97), not missing Marsh's Library (p100), before heading back to town for dinner on the covered terrace at Eden (p70), then a few scoops and some live trad music at the Stag's Head (p94).

DAY TWO

Start amid the manuscripts at the Chester Beatty Library (p79) in Dublin Castle (p79), pit stopping at the Queen of Tarts (p72) for a coffee and a slice of cake. Browse the shops around Grafton St (Map p39) before a visit to the National Museum (p56) or National Gallery (p55). Catch evensong at Christ Church Cathedral (p98) before indulging in a leisurely dinner at L'Gueuleton (p90) and a comedy show at the International Bar (p51).

DAY THREE

Pick up some tasty ethnic food on a stroll around Moore St (Map p105, C2) and Parnell St (Map p105, C2) before dropping into the James Joyce Cultural Centre (p108) for a walking tour or across to Cobalt Café and Gallery (p115) for some warm soda bread and tea. Then head west to the Irish Museum of Modern Art (p99) and Kilmainham Gaol (p100) for a cultural fix. Enjoy an early dinner at Fallon & Byrne (p87) before a show at the Project Arts Centre (p77) in Temple Bar.

Top left Impressively vaulted interior of the Christ Church Cathedral **Top right** Browsing the literary wares in George's St Arcade **Bottom** Warm wood and mint-green walls cocoon art lovers in the National Gallery

ITINERARIES

RAINY DAY

Uncertain, inclement weather has made Dublin a city of interiors. You could spend hours perusing the National Museum (p56) and National Gallery (p55), but don't miss out on the wonderful Chester Beatty Library (p79). A wet-day pick-me-up at the Queen of Tarts (p72) is a must before heading into Temple Bar and visiting the Gallery of Photography (p66). By now, all cultured up, it's time to enjoy the rain like most Dubliners do, with a pint at the pub – the Long Hall (p93) should do the trick.

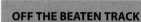

OFF THE BEATEN TRACK
Dublin's centre can get congested with people and cars, but it's not difficult to find some peace. For a real escape head to the seaside suburbs, or try some of the more central idylls:
> Farmleigh's pleasure gardens (p122)
> South Wall walk to the lighthouse (pictured below)
> Prospect Cemetery (p115)
> Outdoor cafe at the Dublin Writers Museum (p107)
> Iveagh Gardens (p54)
> Blessington St City Basin (Map p121, E1)

Vibrantly red, the Poolbeg Lighthouse on the Great South Wall commands attention

FORWARD PLANNING

During summer, queues can be horrendous at popular attractions so try to arrive early. Most fee-paying sights offer discounts to students, seniors, children and families. If you're serious about sightseeing, buy the Dublin Pass (see p162) as soon as you set foot in the airport – it'll give a you free ride on the Aircoach.

Two weeks before you go Advance purchase is a must if you want to take in a hit play at the Abbey Theatre (p118) or the Gate Theatre (p118) – a couple of weeks ahead should be plenty of time. Ditto if you want to watch a game at Croke Park (p114), especially for the latter stages of the championship.

Three days before you go The very best and newest of Dublin's restaurants can be pretty tough to get a table at if you leave it to the last minute, but you shouldn't have any problems if you book a few days in advance.

PINTS APLENTY

How many you have is entirely up to you, but we suggest you kick off your journey into the unknown at the well-hidden Bar With No Name (p91) before going for an artsy pint in atmospheric Grogan's Castle Lounge (p93). From there, stop off at the Long Hall (p93) before walking south into the heart of SoDa. Wexford and Camden Sts have the wonderful Anseo (p91). Back in the city centre, you should at least pop your head into Ron Black's (p50) before heading back towards SoDa and having a drink or two in the Stag's Head (p94). Then – oiled up to the gills – venture into the mayhem of Temple Bar. The Palace Bar (p74) is terrific and, who knows, there might even be a traditional music session on upstairs.

DUBLIN FOR FREE

You can keep your money in your pocket at all of the national museums and galleries, including the superb Irish Museum of Modern Art (p99), but also worth keeping in mind is a visit to the Government Buildings (p54) – pick up your visitor ticket from the National Gallery. You'll have to book in advance, but the tour of Leinster House (p55) – where the parliament sits – is also free, as are, of course, all of the city's Georgian squares. Be sure to take a peek at the Bank of Ireland (p40) on College Green – once home to the first Irish Parliament – before wandering about the evocative campus of Trinity College (p40), perhaps stopping into the Douglas Hyde Gallery (p40).

OPEN--->
FREEBIRD
RECORDS

Dubstep Hip Ho
Drum&Bass Jazz
House Techno
Rock Breakbeat
DJ Tools

>1	Grafton Street & Around	38
>2	Georgian Dublin	52
>3	Temple Bar	64
>4	SoDa	78
>5	Kilmainham & the Liberties	96
>6	O'Connell Street & Around	104
>7	Smithfield & Phoenix Park	120
>8	Beyond the Grand Canal	126

Pedestrians stroll past a music-store mural in Temple Bar (p64)

NEIGHBOURHOODS

A compact city centre with ne'er a hill worthy of the name makes Dublin a dream to get around. Shoe-power is your best mode of transport, especially as the majority of the sights are quite central, while the ones that demand a little legwork are genuinely worth the effort. Unless you're driving – and for God's sake what are you doing that for? – you should breeze through the city, barely putting a dent in your soles.

To make it even easier to navigate, we've divided the city into eight bite-sized chunks – six of them south of the Liffey where most of the tourist life is lived. Grafton Street and around covers the area surrounding Dublin's main recreational thoroughfare, while Temple Bar is its designated tourist heart and SoDa its cutting edge. Kilmainham and the Liberties, to the west of the city centre, are laden with sights and character, but are light on social opportunities, while Georgian Dublin to the east is a large sprawling area surrounding Merrion Sq and St Stephen's Green, and contains many of Ireland's national museums. Further east, beyond the Grand Canal, are the wealthy inner southern suburbs, which harbour some of Dublin's trendiest eateries.

North of the Liffey, O'Connell Street and around showcases the sights and attractions of the city's one-time centre and still its grandest avenue – after years in the doldrums it has redecorated its way back into the spotlight. To the west, Smithfield and Phoenix Park covers the more traditional neighbourhoods and the city's giant-sized park.

For a taste of workaday Dublin, check out the Worth the Trip boxed texts in the O'Connell St chapter to discover some seaside spots to the east and the host of worthwhile sights north of the Royal Canal – not to mention a glimpse of everyday suburban living!

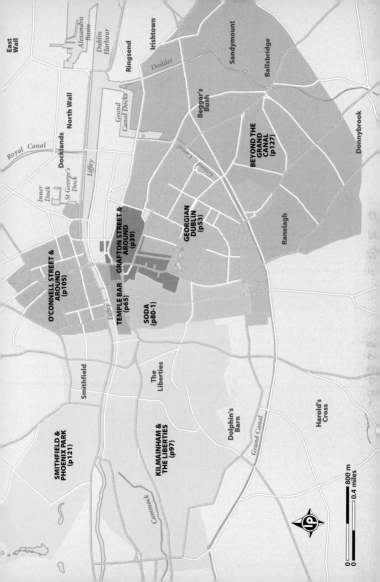

East Wall

Alexandra Basin

Dublin Harbour

Ringsend

Irishtown

Sandymount

Ballsbridge

North Wall

Grand Canal Docks

Dodder

Beggar's Bush

Royal Canal

Docklands

Inner Dock

St George's Dock

Liffey

Grand Canal

Grand Canal

BEYOND THE GRAND CANAL (p127)

Donnybrook

O'CONNELL STREET & AROUND (p105)

GRAFTON STREET & AROUND (p39)

GEORGIAN DUBLIN (p53)

Ranelagh

Liffey

TEMPLE BAR (p65)

SODA (p80-1)

Smithfield

The Liberties

SMITHFIELD & PHOENIX PARK (p121)

KILMAINHAM & THE LIBERTIES (p97)

Dolphin's Barn

Grand Canal

Harold's Cross

Camac

0   800 m
0   0.4 miles

>GRAFTON STREET & AROUND

Dublin's affluent heart is this short, pedestrianised street named after the 17th-century Duke of Grafton, who owned much of these parts before it became the chichi area it is today. At its northern end is College Green, directly in front of the elegant facades of Trinity College (one of the world's most prestigious universities), and the Bank of Ireland (built to house Ireland's first parliament). An unremarkable statue of Molly Malone leads us, bosoms first, to the city's premier shopping thoroughfare, throbbing with all kinds of street life, from bag-laden retail junkies to enthusiastic street performers. Its southern tip leads into leafy St Stephen's Green, Dublin's most popular Georgian square.

GRAFTON STREET & AROUND

◉ SEE
Bank of Ireland 1 C2
Douglas Hyde Gallery 2 D2
Kerlin Gallery 3 C3
Science Gallery 4 F2
Trinity College 5 D2

🛍 SHOP
Alias Tom 6 C3
Angles ....(see 27)
Appleby 7 C3
Avoca Handweavers 8 C2
Brown Thomas 9 C3
BT2 ....10 C3
Cathach Books 11 D3
Chica ....(see 27)
Design Centre ....(see 20)
Designyard 12 D2
Dunnes Stores 13 C3
Great Outdoors 14 C3

H Danker 15 C3
Hodges Figgis 16 D3
Magills 17 C3
Murder Ink 18 D3
Optica 19 C3
Powerscourt Centre ...20 C3
Rhinestones 21 C2
Sheridans
    Cheesemongers 22 C3
Stephen's Green
    Shopping Centre 23 C4
Tommy Hilfiger 24 C2
Waterstone's 25 D3
Weir & Sons 26 C2
Westbury Mall 27 C3

🍴 EAT
Avoca Cafe ....(see 8)
Bleu 28 D4
Eddie Rocket's ....(see 36)
Gotham Café 29 C3

Harry's Cafe 30 D4
Marco Pierre White
    Steakhouse & Grill 31 D3
Nude 32 C2
Steps of Rome 33 C3
Thornton's 34 C4
Trocadero 35 C2

🍸 DRINK
Kehoe's 36 C3
La Cave 37 C3
O'Neill's 38 C2
Ron Black's 39 D3

⭐ PLAY
Bewley's Café Theatre ..40 C3
Gaiety Theatre 41 C3
International Bar 42 C2
Lillies Bordello 43 C2
Screen 44 D1

👁 SEE

🔵 BANK OF IRELAND

☎ 671 1488, 677 6801; www.bank ofireland.ie; College Green; admission free; 🕐 10am-4pm Mon-Wed & Fri, to 5pm Thu; 🚌 all city-centre, 🚉 Tara St

Built for the Irish Parliament, the Bank of Ireland moved in after the Act of Union in 1801. Though the House of Commons was subsequently remodelled, the House of Lords survived intact. Its Irish oak woodwork, mahogany standing clock and tapestries are worth a look. Free tours are held on Tuesday at 10.30am, 11.30am and 1.45pm.

🔵 DOUGLAS HYDE GALLERY

☎ 896 1116; www.douglashyde gallery.com; Trinity College; admission free; 🕐 11am-6pm Mon-Wed & Fri, to 7pm Thu, to 4.45pm Sat; 🚌 all city-centre, 🚉 Pearse, Tara St

This is one of those marvellous galleries that seems to have escaped the public radar, partly because of its location tucked away on campus at Trinity. Its ambitious contemporary program sticks firmly in the cutting-edge camp and exhibitions here are often 'enhanced' with film, live music or performance-driven sideshows.

🔵 KERLIN GALLERY

☎ 670 9093; www.kerlin.ie; Anne's Lane, S Anne St; admission free; 🕐 10am-5.45pm Mon-Fri, 11am-4.30pm Sat; 🚌 10, 14, 14a, 15

Hidden behind a nondescript door in a dingy little lane, the Kerlin Gallery is the ultimate statement in cool. Inside, the minimalist space displays mainly conceptual and abstract art from some of Ireland's leading lights, including Sean Scully and Jaki Irvine.

🔵 SCIENCE GALLERY

☎ 896 4091; www.sciencegallery.ie; admission free; 🕐 exhibitions usually noon-6pm Tue-Sun; 🚌 all city-centre, 🚉 Pearse, Tara St

The city's newest gallery offers a refreshingly lively and informative exploration of the relationship between science, art and the world we live in. Exhibitions are of the hands-on, in-your-face variety, urging you to question your normal surroundings and the assumptions you have about everyday things.

🔵 TRINITY COLLEGE

☎ 896 1000; www.tcd.ie/Library/old -library; grounds free, tour incl Long Room & Book of Kells €10, under 12 free; 🕐 grounds 8am-midnight, Long Room/ Book of Kells 9.30am-5pm Mon-Sat, to 4.30pm Sun, from noon Sun Oct-May; 🚌 all city-centre, 🚉 Pearse, Tara St

Stretching 65m, the Long Room at Trinity College boasts around 200,000 books

The country's most famous university is an oasis of Victorian tranquillity in the middle of the city. Founded by Elizabeth I in 1592, most of the stunning buildings and landscaped squares date from the 18th and 19th centuries, but the campus' single biggest attraction is much, much older – queue up to gape at the *Book of Kells,* one of the world's most extraordinary illuminated manuscripts. Thirty-minute walking tours are available, see website for details. See also p10.

🛒 SHOP

🛍 ALIAS TOM *Men's Clothing*
☎ 671 5443; Duke Lane; 🕑 9.30am-6pm Mon-Wed, Fri & Sat, to 8pm Thu; 🚇 all city-centre, 🚋 St Stephen's Green
This is Dublin's best designer menswear boutique, where friendly staff guide you through casuals by bling labels Burberry and YSL. Downstairs you'll find classic tailored suits and Patrick Cox shoes.

🛍 ANGLES *Jewellery*
☎ 679 1964; Westbury Mall; 🕑 10am-6pm Mon-Wed, Fri & Sat, to 7pm Thu; 🚇 all city-centre, 🚋 St Stephen's Green
You won't find Claddagh rings or charm bracelets here, just cabinets full of handmade, contemporary Irish jewellery, most of it by up-and-coming Dublin craftspeople. Commissions are taken and items can be sent on to you abroad.

🛍 APPLEBY *Jewellery*
☎ 679 9572; 5-6 Johnson's Ct; 🕑 9.30am-5.30pm Mon & Fri, to 7pm Thu, to 6pm Sat; 🚇 all city-centre, 🚋 St Stephen's Green
Renowned for the high quality of its gold and silver jewellery, which

tends towards more conventional designs, this is the place to shop for serious stuff – diamond rings, sapphire-encrusted cufflinks and Raymond Weil watches.

AVOCA HANDWEAVERS
Clothing & Home Decor

☎ 677 4215; 11-13 Suffolk St; ☽ 10am-6pm Mon-Wed, Fri & Sat, to 8pm Thu, 11am-6pm Sun; 🚋 all city-centre

Combining clothing, house wares, a basement food hall and an excellent top-floor cafe, Avoca promotes a stylish but homey brand of modern Irish life. Many of the garments sold here are woven, knitted and naturally dyed at its Wicklow factory. The children's section, which features unusual knits, fairy outfits, bee-covered gumboots and dinky toys, is fantastic.

BROWN THOMAS
Department Store

☎ 605 6666; 95 Grafton St; ☽ 9am-8pm Mon-Wed & Fri, to 9pm Thu, to 7pm Sat, 10am-7pm Sun; 🚋 all city-centre, 🚇 St Stephen's Green

Soak up the Jo Malone–laden rarefied atmosphere of Dublin's most exclusive department store, where presentation is virtually artistic. Here you'll find a selection of fantastic cosmetics, shoes to die for, exotic home wares and a host of Irish and international fashion

The forefront of fashion in a Brown Thomas display

labels such as Balenciaga, Stella McCartney, Lainey Keogh and Philip Treacy.

BT2 *Clothing*

☎ 679 5666; 88 Grafton St; ☽ 9am-6.30pm Mon-Wed & Fri, to 9pm Thu, to 7pm Sat, 10am-6.30pm Sun; 🚋 all city-centre, 🚇 St Stephen's Green

Brown Thomas' young and funky offshoot, with high-end casuals for men and women, and a juice bar upstairs overlooking Grafton St. Brands include DKNY, Custom, Ted Baker, Diesel and Tommy Hilfiger.

CATHACH BOOKS *Books*

☎ 671 8676; 10 Duke St; ☽ 9.30am-5.45pm Mon-Sat; 🚋 all city-centre

Dusty rare editions of Irish litera-ture and history, including works by Wilde, Joyce, Yeats and Beckett, and a large selection of signed first editions await you in one of Dub-lin's best antiquarian bookshops.

🏠 CHICA *Women's Clothing*
☎ 633 4441; Westbury Mall; 🕑 10am-6pm Tue, Wed, Fri & Sat, to 7pm Thu; 🚌 all city-centre, 🚊 St Stephen's Green
A one-stop shop for all your chic party needs. This little boutique will sort out your wardrobe with wow-factor dresses from Sika, Ugo Zaldi or its own Chica Boutique label.

🏠 DESIGN CENTRE
Women's Clothing
☎ 679 5718; Powerscourt Centre; 🕑 10am-6pm Mon-Wed & Fri, to 8pm Thu, 9.30am-6pm Sat; 🚌 all city-centre, 🚊 St Stephen's Green
Mostly dedicated to Irish designer women's wear, with well-made, classic suits, evening wear and knitwear. Irish labels include N&C Kilkenny, Pauric Sweeney, Roisin Linnane and Philip Treacy. Ben De Lisi, Ophelie and La Petite Salope also get a look in.

🏠 DESIGNYARD
Jewellery, Arts & Crafts
☎ 474 1011; 48-49 Nassau St; 🕑 9.30am-6.30pm Mon-Wed & Fri, to 8pm Thu, 9am-6.30pm Sat, 10am-6pm Sun; 🚌 all city-centre

A high-end, craft-as-art shop where everything you see – glass, batik, sculpture, painting – is one-off and handmade in Ireland. It also show-cases contemporary jewellery stock from young international designers.

🏠 DUNNES STORES
Department Store
☎ 671 4629; 62 Grafton St; 🕑 9am-6.30pm Mon-Wed, Fri & Sat, to 9pm Thu, noon-6pm Sun; 🚌 all city-centre, 🚊 St Stephen's Green
A favourite choice with Irish families for its affordable everyday clothing. The Savida fashion range is remarkably on the pulse, though, and has an excellent homewares department. Look for branches across the city.

🏠 GREAT OUTDOORS
Outdoor Gear
☎ 679 4293; 20 Chatham St; 🕑 9.30am-5.30pm Mon-Wed, Fri & Sat, to 8pm Thu; 🚌 all city-centre, 🚊 St Stephen's Green
Dublin's best outdoors store, with gear for hiking, camping, surfing, mountaineering, swimming and more. Also has an info-laden noticeboard.

🏠 H DANKER
Antiques & Jewellery
☎ 677 4009; 10 S Anne St; 🕑 9.30am-5pm Mon-Sat; 🚌 all city-centre
Chock-full of exquisite treasures, this shop specialises in Irish and

English antique silver, jewellery and objets d'art.

📷 HODGES FIGGIS *Books*
☎ 677 4754; 57 Dawson St; ⏰ 9am-7pm Mon-Wed & Fri, to 8pm Thu, to 6pm Sat, noon-6pm Sun; 🚌 all city-centre
The most complete bookshop in town has books on every conceivable subject for every kind of reader. A very wide range of Irish-interest titles is found on the ground floor.

📷 MAGILLS *Gourmet Food*
☎ 671 3830; 14 Clarendon St; ⏰ 9.30am-5.45pm Mon-Sat; 🚌 all city-centre, 🚇 St Stephen's Green
With its characterful old facade and tiny dark interior, Magills' old-world charm reminds you how Clarendon St must have once looked. Family-run, you get the distinct feeling that every Irish and French cheese, olive oil, packet of Italian pasta and salami has been hand-picked.

📷 MURDER INK *Books*
☎ 677 7570; 15 Dawson St; ⏰ 10am-5.30pm Mon-Sat, noon-5pm Sun; 🚌 all city-centre, 🚇 St Stephen's Green
All manner of murder mystery and crime novels are available in this specialist bookshop that has categorisation down to a fine art – choose from historical mystery, romantic crime, sci-fi mystery, true crime and more.

📷 OPTICA *Accessories*
☎ 677 4705; 1 Royal Hibernian Way; ⏰ 9.30am-5.30pm Mon-Wed, Fri & Sat, to 6.30pm Thu; 🚌 all city-centre, 🚇 St Stephen's Green
Who says guys don't make passes at girls who wear glasses? Knock 'em dead in head-turning specs and shades by Chanel, D&G, Stella McCartney and Oliver Peoples.

📷 POWERSCOURT CENTRE *Shopping Centre*
☎ 679 4144; 59 S William St; ⏰ 10am-6pm Mon-Wed & Fri, to 8pm Thu, 9am-6pm Sat, noon-6pm Sun; 🚌 all city-centre, 🚇 St Stephen's Green
This upmarket shopping mall in an 18th-century town house is where discerning shoppers quietly visit boutiques, beauty salons and the 1st-floor art, craft and antique shops. The Design Centre and FCUK are also here, as is a great vegetarian restaurant and a wig store. The courtyard Powerscourt Cafe is a pleasant spot to gather yourself.

📷 RHINESTONES *Jewellery*
☎ 679 0759; 18 St Andrew's St; ⏰ 9am-6.30pm Mon-Wed, Fri & Sat, to 8pm Thu, noon-6pm Sun; 🚌 all city-centre
Exceptionally fine antique and quirky costume jewellery from the 1920s to 1970s, with pieces priced from €25 to €2000. Victorian jet, 1950s enamel, art-deco turquoise,

1930s mother-of-pearl, cut-glass and rhinestone necklaces, bracelets, brooches and rings are displayed by colour in old-fashioned cabinets.

🏠 SHERIDANS CHEESEMONGERS
Gourmet Food

☎ 679 3143; 11 S Anne St; 🕐 10am-6pm Mon-Fri, from 9.30am Sat; 🚌 all city-centre, 🚇 St Stephen's Green

If heaven were a cheese shop, this would be it. Wooden shelves are laden with rounds of farmhouse cheeses, sourced by Kevin and Seamus Sheridan, who have almost single-handedly revived the practice of cheese-making in Ireland. You can taste any one of the 60 cheeses on display and, while you're at it, you can also pick up some wild Irish salmon, Italian pastas and olives.

🏠 STEPHEN'S GREEN SHOPPING CENTRE
Shopping Centre

☎ 478 0888; cnr S King St & W St Stephen's Green; 🕐 9am-6pm Mon-Wed, Fri & Sat, to 9pm Thu, noon-6pm Sun; 🚌 all city-centre, 🚇 St Stephen's Green

A 1980s version of a 19th-century shopping arcade, the dramatic, balconied interior and central courtyard are a bit too grand for the nondescript chain stores

The dramatic light-filled interior of Stephen's Green Shopping Centre

NEIGHBOURHOODS

GRAFTON STREET & AROUND

Cheeses galore inside Sheridans (p45)

within. Here you'll find a Boots, Benetton and large Dunnes Store with supermarket, as well as last-season designer warehouse TK Maxx.

🄲 TOMMY HILFIGER *Clothing*
☎ 633 7010; 13-14 Grafton St; ☸ 9.30am-7pm Mon-Tue, to 8pm Wed & Fri, to 9pm Thu, 9am-7pm Sat, 11am-6pm Sun; 🚌 all city-centre, 🚊 St Stephen's Green

'Traditional with a twist' is how Tommy Hilfiger describes his own fashions, and he's right, if the twist is designing clothes that are as appealing to a yummy mummy as to a rapper. The American designer cut the ribbon on this elegant

store on Dublin's most prestigious shopping street in late 2008.

🄲 WATERSTONE'S *Books*
☎ 679 1415; 7 Dawson St; ☸ 9am-7pm Mon-Wed & Fri, to 8pm Thu, to 6.30pm Sat, noon-6pm Sun; 🚌 all city-centre

Although it is large and multi-storied, Waterstone's somehow manages to maintain that hide-in-a-corner ambience that book lovers adore. The broad selection of books is supplemented by five bookcases of Irish fiction, in addition to poetry, drama, politics and history. Waterstone's hosts book signings every Thursday evening; check the board outside for details.

🄲 WEIR & SONS *Jewellery*
☎ 677 9678; 96-99 Grafton St; ☸ 9am-5.30pm Mon-Wed, Fri & Sat, to 8pm Thu; 🚌 all city-centre

ARMCHAIR SHOPPING
Want to avoid the leg-numbing march of the pavements in search of a bargain or much sought-after souvenir? Relax, grab a cuppa and do it online.
> www.buy4now.ie – A catch-all website of Irish shops that offers nearly everything you can think of, from ski holidays to boxed sets of *Fair City*.
> www.shopirishwithmoytura.com – Irish-themed items include bodhráns (Irish drums), Paddy's day souvenirs and Irish biscuits.

The largest jeweller in Ireland, this huge store on Grafton St first opened in 1869 and still has its original wooden cabinets and a workshop on the premises. There's new and antique Irish jewellery (including Celtic designs) and a huge selection of watches, Irish crystal, porcelain, leather and travel goods.

🏠 WESTBURY MALL
Shopping Centre
Clarendon St; 🕙 **10am-6pm Mon-Sat, noon-5pm Sun;** 🚌 **all city-centre, 🚇 St Stephen's Green**
Wedged between the five-star Westbury Hotel and the expensive jewellery stores of Johnson's Ct, this small mall has a handful of pricey, specialist shops selling everything from Persian rugs to buttons and lace or tasteful wooden children's toys.

🍴 EAT

🍴 AVOCA CAFE *Cafe* €€
☎ **672 6019; www.avoca.ie; Avoca Handweavers, 11-13 Suffolk St;** 🕙 **10am-5pm Mon-Sat, from 10.30am Sun;** 🚌 **all city-centre;** 🆅 🚼
This airy cafe was one of Dublin's best-kept secrets – hidden above Avoca Handweavers (p42) – until discovered by the shopping jet set. Battle your way to a table past the designer shopping bags, where you'll relish the rustic,

delicious delights of organic shepherd's pie, roast lamb with couscous, or sumptuous salads. There's a secret takeaway salad bar and hot counter in the basement.

🍴 BLEU *Modern Irish* €€€
☎ **676 7015; www.bleu.ie; Joshua House, Dawson St;** 🕙 **noon-3pm & 6-11pm;** 🚇 **St Stephen's Green;** 🆅
With black leather seats and massive windows overlooking swanky Dawson St, you can see and be seen at Eamon O'Reilly's upmarket outpost of modern Irish cuisine. Confit of pork belly, wild mushroom and tarragon risotto and – that trademark of trendy menus – a ground rib eye burger keep upmarket-preclubber's hunger pangs at bay for a few hours.

🍴 GOTHAM CAFÉ *Pizza* €€
☎ **679 5266; www.gothamcafe.ie; 8 S Anne St;** 🕙 **noon-midnight Mon-Sat, noon-10.30pm Sun;** 🚇 **St Stephen's Green;** 🆅 🚼
A vibrant, youthful place that is decorated with framed Rolling Stones album covers, Gotham extends its New York theme to its delicious pizzas named after districts in the Big Apple. Chinatown and Noho are among our favourites, or you can opt for pasta, crostini or Asian salads. And, hey, they love kids here.

🍴 HARRY'S CAFE *Cafe* €€

☎ 639 4889; www.harryscafe.ie; 22 Dawson St; ☼ noon-4pm Mon, to 11pm Tue-Sat, to 10.30pm Sun; 🚌 all city-centre, 🚊 St Stephen's Green; V ♿

Harry's has some great drops on the wine list, many of which you'll see mounted on the bare brick walls of this friendly place. House specialities include organic beef burgers or bangers and mash, but the baked Mediterranean stack oozing melted goat's cheese is our favourite.

🍴 MARCO PIERRE WHITE STEAKHOUSE & GRILL

Steakhouse €€€

☎ 677 1155; www.fitzers.ie; 51 Dawson St; ☼ noon-11pm; 🚊 St Stephen's Green

The long-established Fitzer's restaurant group scored quite a coup when they enlisted bad boy chef Marco Pierre White (he who once made Gordon Ramsey cry) to lend his name to their newest venture, which opened in 2009. Steaks, grilled meats and chunks of fish are the fare, presented with a minimum of fuss, but with plenty of flavour.

🍴 NUDE *Cafe* €

☎ 677 4804; www.nude.ie; 21 Suffolk St; ☼ 8am-9pm Mon-Wed, Fri & Sat, to 9.30pm Thu, to 7pm Sun; 🚌 all city-centre; V

Long-table dining in the Powerscourt Centre (p44)

CONSUMER R&R

There's no need to shop till you drop while pounding the streets of Dublin. Several stores have quiet and comfortable cafes where you can refuel, take stock and plan your next move.

> Avoca Handweavers (p47)
> Brown Thomas (p42)
> Kilkenny (p59)
> Powerscourt Centre (p44)
> Winding Stair (p116)

With juice bars a-go-go in the city, modernist Nude may no longer be the rarity it once was, but it still maintains its own unique identity. Owned by Bono's brother, it takes the fast-food experience to a delicious and healthy extreme offering hot Asian wraps, bean casseroles and spirulina-spiked juices to go or have on the (plastic-free) spot.

🍽 STEPS OF ROME *Italian* €

☎ 670 5630; Chatham St; 🕑 10am-midnight; 🚌 all city-centre, 🚊 St Stephen's Green

One of the best open secrets in town is this tiny kerbside cafe just off Grafton St, where you can take away rustic pizza slices or sit in and rub elbows with the Italian frat pack over as authentic a bowl of pasta as you'll find anywhere. It's always jammed and you can't book, but service is smart so you'll usually get a table after a few minutes' wait.

🍽 THORNTON'S

Modern European €€€

☎ 478 7008; www.thorntonsrestaurant.com; Fitzwilliam Hotel, 128 W St Stephen's Green; 🕑 12.30-2pm & 7-10pm Tue-Sat; 🚌 all city-centre, 🚊 St Stephen's Green

Kevin Thornton may have lost one of his two Michelin stars a few years ago, but he has proved

somewhat defiantly that Michelin's loss was his customer's gain, and his mouth-watering interpretation of modern French cuisine is as superb as ever. Faultless service, gorgeous room overlooking St Stephen's Green…want to watch a grown-up squirm? Ask for ketchup.

🍽 TROCADERO

Traditional Irish €€€

☎ 677 5545; www.trocadero.ie; 4 St Andrew's St; 🕑 5pm-midnight Mon-Sat; 🚌 all city-centre

There used to be a time when the Troc was the only place in town for a splash-out celebratory meal, hopefully alongside the glitterati of Dublin's screens and stages. No more, but old school thespians, hacks, musos and TV execs are still partial to this warm and friendly art-deco restaurant that won't challenge your taste buds but rarely fails to deliver old favourites.

🍸 DRINK

🍸 KEHOE'S *Pub*

☎ 677 8312; 9 S Anne St; 🚍 all city-centre
One of Dublin's most atmospheric pubs, featuring a beautiful Victorian bar, Kehoe's has comfy snugs and plenty of other little nooks and crannies in which to secrete yourself. Upstairs, drinks are served in what was once the publican's living room – and it looks it.

🍸 LA CAVE *Wine Bar*

☎ 679 4409; 28 S Anne St; 🕑 12.30pm-late Mon-Sat, 6pm-late Sun; 🚍 all city-centre, 🚊 St Stephen's Green
From the outside, La Cave looks like it might be an adult bookshop or a gangster pool hall. Wind your way downstairs and you'll discover a chic, Paris-style wine bar with crimson walls, tiny tables and a packed crowd shouting over the Brazilian salsa music. The food is OK, but you're really here for the setting and the superb wine list.

🍸 O'NEILL'S *Pub*

☎ 679 3671; 2 Suffolk St; 🚍 all city-centre
A labyrinthine old pub situated near Trinity College, O'Neill's dates from the late 19th century, though a tavern has stood on this site for more than 300 years. The odd combination of students and stockbrokers lends the place a chaotic air and it offers good food, too.

🍸 RON BLACK'S *Pub*

☎ 672 8231; 37 Dawson St; 🕑 11am-11.30pm Mon-Wed, to 2am Thu-Sat, noon-11pm Sun; 🚍 10, 14, 14a, 15
Despite its cavernous size, this upmarket watering hole manages to retain an inviting atmosphere, thanks to plenty of warm wooden panelling, leather sofas and huge soft lights. The newly opened champagne bar upstairs attracts be-suited young men and smart-dressed girls who aren't afraid to flash their cash.

⭐ PLAY

⭐ BEWLEY'S CAFÉ THEATRE
Performances

☎ 086 878 4001; www.bewleyscafe theatre.com; 78-79 Grafton St; admission €8-15; 🕑 12.50pm & 8.30pm; 🚊 St Stephen's Green; ♿
The theatre space in the beautiful Oriental Room at Bewley's Café is long established for its excellent lunchtime drama (admission includes soup and sandwich) as well as an evening program featuring rigorous drama, comedy and jazz.

⭐ GAIETY THEATRE
Performances

☎ 677 1717; www.gaietytheatre.com; S King St; admission €10-20; 🕑 box office 10am-7pm Mon-Sat; 🚍 all city-centre, 🚊 St Stephen's Green; ♿

Opened in 1871, this Victorian theatre was restored to its former glory several years ago. Its repertoire is diverse, from modern plays, musicals, comedies and panto to Shakespeare. Opera Ireland has a season here. On Friday and Saturday nights the venue is taken over by salsa and soul clubs until 4am.

⭐ INTERNATIONAL BAR
Comedy
☎ 677 9250; www.international-bar
.com; 23 Wicklow St; admission €10/8;
🕙 comedy Mon, Wed-Sat 9pm;
🚌 all city-centre

A fantastic pub with stained glass and mirrors, famous for its long-running comedy nights and jazz and blues on Tuesday. Ardal O'Hanlon, who played Dougal in *Father Ted*, began his career here doing stand-up, as did TV comics Dara O'Briain and Des Bishop.

⭐ LILLIES BORDELLO *Club*
☎ 679 9204; www.lilliesbordello.ie;
Adam Ct; admission €10-20;
🕙 11pm-3am; 🚌 all city-centre

Lillies is strictly for wannabes, Big Hairs and visiting rock stars. Don't think you'll get to rub shoulders with the celebs though, as they'll be whisked out of view and into

A comic delivers her lines at the International Bar

the VIP room in a flash. As you might expect, the music is mostly safe and commercial.

⭐ SCREEN *Cinema*
☎ 672 5500; 2 Townsend St;
admission before/after 6pm €6.50/8.50;
🕙 2-10.30pm; 🚌 5, 7, 7a, 8, 14,
🚊 Tara St; ♿

Between Trinity College and O'Connell Bridge, Screen shows fairly good art-house and indie films on its three screens.

>GEORGIAN DUBLIN

Moneyed Dublin works and plays east of Grafton St, amid the magnificent Georgian splendour thrown up during Dublin's 18th-century prime. However, it wasn't always thus: until the mid-18th century, fashionable Dublin resided firmly on the north side of the Liffey, and when James Fitzgerald, the earl of Kildare, built his mansion south of the Liffey, he was mocked for his foolhardy move into the wilds. But Jimmy Fitz had a nose for real estate: 'Where I go society will follow', he confidently predicted, and he was soon proved right; today Leinster House is used as the Irish Parliament and is in the epicentre of Georgian Dublin, so named because the construction boom coincided roughly with the reign of the four Georges on the English throne (1714–1830). This area has museums, fine houses, landscaped squares and some of the best restaurants in the city.

GEORGIAN DUBLIN

☻ SEE
Fitzwilliam Square **1** D3
Government Buildings ..**2** D2
Irish-Jewish Museum **3** A4
Iveagh Gardens **4** C3
Leinster House **5** C1
Merrion Square **6** D2
National Gallery of
  Ireland **7** D1
National Library **8** C1
National Museum of
  Ireland – Archaeology ..**9** C1
Newman House **10** C2
Newman University
  Church **11** B2
Number 29 ....**12** E2
Origin Gallery **13** B3
RHA Gallagher Gallery ..**14** C2
Royal Institute of the
  Architects of Ireland
  (RIA) **15** E1

St Stephen's
  Church **16** E2
St Stephen's Green **17** C2
Taylor Galleries **18** C2

☐ SHOP
Cleo **19** C2
Kilkenny **20** C1
Mitchell & Son Wine
  Merchants **21** C2

⊪ EAT
Bang Café **22** C2
Bentley's Oyster Bar
  & Grill **23** C2
Canal Bank Café **24** D4
Dax **25** C3
Dunne & Crescenzi **26** C1
Ely **27** C2
L'Ecrivain **28** D2

Restaurant Patrick
  Guilbaud **29** D2
Shanahan's on the
  Green **30** B2
Town Bar & Grill **31** C2
Unicorn **32** C2

☒ DRINK
Doheny & Nesbitt's **33** D2
O'Donoghue's **34** D2
Toner's **35** D2

★ PLAY
National Concert Hall ..**36** C3
Renard's **37** C1
Sugar Club **38** C3

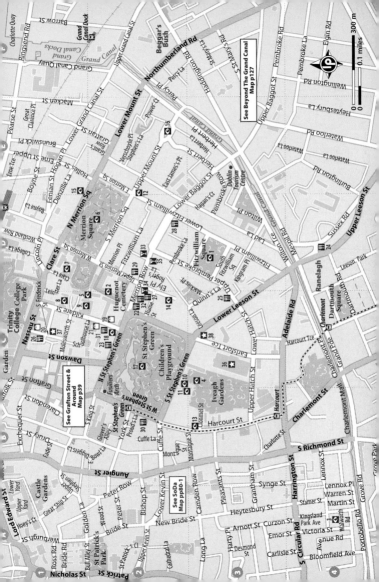

👁 SEE

👁 FITZWILLIAM SQUARE
📍 10, 11, 13b, 46a, 5

The smallest and last of Dublin's great Georgian squares, Fitzwilliam is home to a quiet and elegant block of immaculate terraces, boasting some elaborate doors and fanlights. While by day the square houses doctors' surgeries and solicitors' offices, by night prostitutes await custom. Only residents have access to the central garden.

👁 GOVERNMENT BUILDINGS
☎ 662 4888; www.taoiseach.gov.ie; Upper Merrion St; admission free, tickets available from National Gallery on day of visit; 🕐 tours 10.30am-1.30pm Sat; 🚌 7, 7a, 8, 45, 🚉 Pearse

The domed Government Buildings, built in an Edwardian interpretation of the Georgian style, were opened originally in 1911 as the Royal College of Science. The tour takes in the office of the taoiseach (prime minister), the cabinet room, ceremonial staircase with a stunning stained-glass window designed by Evie Hone (1894–1955) for the 1939 New York Trade Fair, and modern Irish arts and crafts.

👁 IRISH-JEWISH MUSEUM
☎ 453 1797; 4 Walworth Rd; admission free; 🕐 11am-3.30pm Tue, Thu & Sun May-Sep, 10.30am-2.30pm Sun Oct-Apr; 🚌 14, 15, 16, 19, 83, 122

Dublin's dwindling Jewish population is remembered through paintings, photographs, certificates, books and other memorabilia in this terrace house in the former Jewish district of Portobello. The museum recreates a typical 19th-century Dublin kosher kitchen, while upstairs is an old synagogue, in a state of disuse since the 1970s.

👁 IVEAGH GARDENS
☎ 475 7816; www.heritageireland.ie; Clonmel St; admission free; 🕐 8am-dusk Mon-Sat, from 10am Sun; 🚌 14, 14a, 15a, 15b, 🚉 Harcourt

Once known to locals as the Secret Garden, the word is out about the beautiful and ramshackle Iveagh Gardens, situated just behind Newman House. Accessible from either Earlsfort Tce or Harcourt St, and less crowded than nearby St Stephen's Green, the gardens

BY GEORGE

The Georgian period is roughly defined as the years between the accession of George I in 1714 and the death of George IV in 1830. Its inspiration was the work of the 16th-century Italian architect Andrea Palladio, who believed reason and the principles of classical antiquity should govern building.

In Dublin, the austere formality of the style was tempered by the use of coloured doors, delicate fanlights, intricate ironwork and exuberant interior plasterwork.

One of Iveagh Gardens' many statues

were designed by Ninian Niven in 1863. Features of the beautifully landscaped gardens include a wonderfully rustic grotto, cascade, fountain, maze and rose garden.

🞂 LEINSTER HOUSE
☎ 618 3000, tour information 618 3271; www.oireachtas.ie; Kildare St; admission free; 🕑 observation gallery 2.30-8.30pm Tue, 10.30am-8.30pm Wed, 10.30am-5.30pm Thu Nov-May;
🚌 7, 7a, 8, 10, 11, 13, 🚆 Pearse
Dublin's grandest Georgian home, built by Richard Cassels between 1745 and 1748 for the intrepid James Fitzgerald, earl of Kildare, has been home to the Dáil and Seanad – the two houses of the

Irish parliament – since 1925. The Kildare St frontage is intended to look like a town house, while from Merrion St it appears to look like a country estate. The White House in the United States, designed by Irish architect James Hoban, was allegedly modelled on its design. Guided tours are available when parliament is not in session – see website for details.

🞂 MERRION SQUARE
🚌 5, 7, 7a, 8, 45; 🚆 Pearse
Merrion Square is lined with stately Georgian buildings whose doors and door knockers, foot-scrapers and peacock fanlights epitomise the elegance of the era. Former residents include the Wilde family, WB Yeats and Daniel O'Connell. Its lush central gardens are perfect for a picnic or peaceful pit stop.

🞂 NATIONAL GALLERY OF IRELAND
☎ 661 5133; www.nationalgallery.ie; W Merrion Sq; admission free;
🕑 9.30am-5.30pm Mon-Wed, Fri & Sat, 9.30am-8.30pm Thu, noon-5.30pm Sun;
🚌 5, 7, 7a, 10, 13a, 44c, 48a, 🚆 Pearse
The collection at the National Gallery is made up of nearly 13,000 paintings, sketches, prints and sculptures, including such highlights as Caravaggio's *The Taking of Christ* and the impressive Beit Collection, made up of a huge inventory of masterpieces by Vermeer,

NEIGHBOURHOODS

GEORGIAN DUBLIN

NATIONAL GALLERY UNMISSABLES
> *The Liffey Swim*, Jack B Yeats
> *Lady Writing a Letter*, Vermeer
> *The Cottage Girl*, Gainsborough
> *Still Life with Mandolin*, Picasso

Velázquez and Goya. Our favourites, however, are the paintings by William's brother Jack B Yeats.

🄲 NATIONAL LIBRARY
☎ 603 0200; www.nli.ie; Kildare St; admission free; 🕑 10am-9pm Mon-Wed, 10am-5pm Thu & Fri, 10am-1pm Sat; 🚌 10, 11, 13

Soak up the atmosphere of the library's gorgeous domed reading room (mentioned in Joyce's *Ulysses*). The extensive collection includes early manuscripts, first editions, maps and other items of interest. Temporary exhibitions are often held on the ground floor; the second floor is home to the Genealogical Office.

🄲 NATIONAL MUSEUM OF IRELAND – ARCHAEOLOGY
☎ 677 7444; www.museum.ie; Kildare St; admission free; 🕑 10am-5pm Tue-Sat, 2-5pm Sun; 🚌 7, 7a, 10, 25x, 39x, 51d, 51x, 🚆 Pearse

Inside the Palladian-style National Museum, with its massive domed rotunda, classical marble columns and ornate mosaic ceilings and floors, you'll find a bounty of Bronze Age gold, Iron Age Celtic metalwork, Viking artefacts and ancient Egyptian relics. Call ahead for family programs on weekends.

Embark on a *Ulysses* pilgrimage to the domed National Library reading room

THE DEAD ZOO

At the time of writing, the **Natural History Museum** (☎ 677 7444; www .museum.ie; Merrion St), nicknamed the 'Dead Zoo' on account of its wonderful collection of stuffed animals and mounted heads, was closed for a refurbishment and will not reopen until 2011.

◉ NEWMAN HOUSE

☎ 716 7422; 85-86 S St Stephen's Green; admission €5/4; ☉ tours noon, 2pm, 3pm & 4pm Tue-Fri Jun-Aug; 🚌 10, 11, 13, 14, 15a, 🚊 St Stephen's Green

Part of University College Dublin, Newman House consists of two exquisitely restored Georgian town houses with spectacular 18th-century stucco interiors. Don't miss the Apollo Room and the Saloon by Paolo and Filippo Lafranchini, and later work by Robert West. Former students of Newman House include writer James Joyce and former president Eamon de Valera.

◉ NEWMAN UNIVERSITY CHURCH

☎ 478 0616; 83 S St Stephen's Green; ☉ 8am-6pm Mon-Sat; 🚌 10, 11, 13, 14, 14a, 15a, 15b

This Catholic church was built between 1854 and 1856 in an elaborate Byzantine style with multicoloured marble and copious gold leaf, making it very fashionable for society weddings. Cardinal Newman, who founded the city's first Catholic university next door at Newman House, is honoured with a bust.

◉ NUMBER 29

☎ 702 6165; www.esb.ie; 29 Lower Fitzwilliam St; admission €5/2.50; ☉ 10am-5pm Tue-Sat, 1-5pm Sun, closed 2 weeks before Christmas; 🚌 6, 7, 10, 45, 🚊 Pearse

Built in 1794 for the widow of a wine merchant, Number 29 reconstructs genteel Dublin home life from 1790 to 1820. Discover how Georgians bathed twice yearly and how ladies used a latter-day mini gym, the leather exercise horse. See the discreet dining-room mirrors that allowed servants to respond to orders without listening in to round-table gossip. The 30-minute tour is a fascinating taste of the city's social history.

◉ ORIGIN GALLERY

☎ 478 5159; 83 Harcourt St; admission free; ☉ 10am-5pm Mon-Fri, noon-4pm Sat; 🚌 14, 15, 16, 19, 🚊 Harcourt

A relaxed space on the 1st floor of a Georgian terrace, Origin functions primarily as a showcase for artists who've stayed at the gallery's County Kerry retreat, Cill Rialaig, and emerging artists putting on their first show. In a similarly encouraging spirit, buyers can pay in instalments.

🄲 RHA GALLAGHER GALLERY

☎ 661 2558; www.royalhibernian
academy.com; 25 Ely Pl; admission free;
🕒 11am-5pm Tue-Sat, from 2pm Sun;
🚌 10, 11, 13b, 51x

Established in 1823, the Royal
Hibernian Academy has five galleries in a large modernist space.
Three of the galleries are dedicated
to curated exhibits featuring a
range of Irish and international
visual art, while the ground-floor
Ashford Gallery promotes the work
of Academy members and artists
who haven't yet secured commercial representation, and the Dr
Tony Ryan Gallery has private and
public collections.

🄲 ROYAL INSTITUTE OF ARCHITECTS OF IRELAND

☎ 676 1703; www.riai.ie; 8 N Merrion
Sq; admission free; 🕒 9.30am-5pm
Mon-Fri; 🚌 5, 7, 27x, 44, 45

The gallery at this headquarters is
host to specialist exhibitions that
will excite anyone with an interest
in building design. Irish and international shows have ranged in topic
from ethnic minority architecture to
Irish footpaths. The institute's own
awards show reflects the changing
face of Irish building.

🄲 ST STEPHEN'S CHURCH

☎ 288 0663; Mount St Cres; 🕒 services
only, 11am Sun; 🚌 5, 7, 7a, 8, 45, 46,
🚆 Grand Canal Dock

MUSIC OF THE GODS

Many of Dublin's churches have accom-
plished choirs that make full use of the
heavenly acoustics.

> Christ Church Cathedral (p98) –
come to hear choral evensong four
times a week.
> St Patrick's Cathedral (p102) – hear
the choir sing evensong and try
to book for the carols performed
around Christmas.
> St Stephen's Church (left) – the
acoustics in the 'Pepper Canister
Church' are superb.

Built in 1825 in Greek Revival style,
St Stephen's is commonly known
as the Pepper Canister Church because of its shape. It hosts classical
concerts from time to time.

🄲 ST STEPHEN'S GREEN

admission free; 🕒 8am-dusk Mon-Sat;
🚆 Pearse, 🚆 St Stephen's Green

While enjoying the nine landscaped hectares of Dublin's most
popular square, consider that
once upon a time this was an
open common used for public
whippings, beatings and hangings. Activities in the green have
quietened since then and are
generally confined to the lunch-
time-picnic-and-stroll variety.
Still, on a summer's day it is the
favourite retreat of office workers,
visitors and lovers alike, who come
to breathe a little fresh air, feed

Vibrant colours and verdant grass – St Stephen's Green is perfect for a leisurely stroll

the ducks and cuddle on the grass. See also p14.

TAYLOR GALLERIES
☎ 676 6055; 16 Kildare St; admission free; 🕒 10am-5.30pm Mon-Fri, 11am-3pm Sat; 🚇 10, 11, 13, 🚆 Pearse
Founded in 1978, Taylor Galleries is the original of the pack. Housed in a fine Georgian building, it shows Ireland's top contemporary artists like Louis le Brocquy, Helen Comerford, James O'Connor and Brian Bourke to a well-heeled clientele.

🛍 SHOP
CLEO *Clothing*
☎ 676 1421; 18 Kildare St; 🕒 9am-5.30pm Mon-Sat; 🚇 11, 11a, 14, 14a, 15a, 🚆 St Stephen's Green

Home-knits and hand-weaves from all over the country (including a fine selection of Aran sweaters) make up the bulk of this shop's collection. The patterns are all very Irish – some more than others; there are sweaters with replicas of Celtic stones and other ancient patterns.

🏠 KILKENNY *Arts & Crafts*
☎ 677 7066; 5-6 Nassau St; 🕒 8.30am-6pm Mon-Wed & Fri, to 8pm Thu, to 6pm Sat, 11am-6pm Sun; 🚇 all city-centre
A large, long-running repository for contemporary, innovative Irish crafts, including multicoloured, modern Irish knits, designer clothing, Orla Kiely bags and some lovely silver jewellery. The beautiful glassware and pottery is sourced from workshops around the country. A great place for presents.

GEORGIAN DUBLIN

⬛ MITCHELL & SON WINE MERCHANTS *Wine*

☎ 676 0766; 21 Kildare St; ⏰ 9am-5.30pm Mon-Fri, from 10.30am Sat; 🚌 11, 11a, 14, 14a, 15a, 🚆 St Stephen's Green
Established in 1805, the store is still run by a sixth- and seventh-generation Mitchell father-and-son team. Wines, champagnes, Irish whiskey and Cuban cigars fill the cavernous space. You can also buy stylish wine racks, glasses, hip flasks and ice buckets.

🍴 EAT
🍴 BANG CAFÉ
Modern European €€€

☎ 676 0898; www.bangrestaurant.com; 11 Merrion Row; ⏰ 12.30-3pm & 6.30-10.30pm Mon-Sat; 🚌 10, 11, 13b, 51
Bang Café has justifiably earned a Bib Gourmand (good food at moderate prices) from those Michelin folks. The modern European grub – created by chef Lorcan Cribbin (ex-Ivy in London, don't you know) – is sharp, tasty and much in demand. Thai baked sea bass, medallions of beef and melt-in-your-mouth roast scallops are just a selection. Reservations are essential.

🍴 BENTLEY'S OYSTER BAR & GRILL *Modern Irish* €€€

☎ 638 3939; www.bentleysdublin.com; 22 St Stephen's Green; ⏰ noon-2.30pm & 6-11pm Mon-Sat, noon-4pm & 6-10pm Sun

Chef Richard Corrigan's greatly successful interpretation of the London original has a menu with a modern Irish theme, but don't forget the oyster bar, where you can have a selection of shucked delights from Galway or Carlingford presented in a variety of ways.

🍴 CANAL BANK CAFÉ
Bistro €€€

☎ 664 2135; www.canalbankcafe.com; 146 Upper Leeson St; ⏰ 10am-11pm, from 11am Sat & Sun; 🚌 11, 46, 118
Life is good at Trevor Browne's airy American-French style bistro, just off the canal. *Moules frites* share the menu with burgers and fish and chips, but there's nothing mundane about the quality of the cuisine, which is uniformly excellent. Prices are the same, day and evening.

🍴 DAX *French* €€€

☎ 676 1494; www.dax.ie; 23 Upper Pembroke St; ⏰ noon-2.15pm Tue-Fri, 6-11pm Tue-Sat; 🚌 10, 11, 46b
Olivier Meisonnave, convivial ex–maître d' of Thornton's, stepped out on his own with Irish chef Pól Óhéannraich to open this posh, rustic restaurant named after his home town, north of Biarritz. Located in a bright basement, it's a place where serious foodies can sate their palate on sea bass with celeriac purée, pork wrapped in serrano ham or truffle risotto.

🍽 DUNNE & CRESCENZI

Italian Wine Bar €

☎ 675 9892; www.dunneandcrescenzi
.com; 14-16 S Frederick St; 🕙 9am-7pm
Mon & Tue, to 10pm Wed-Sat; 🚍 all
city-centre; Ⓥ ♿

This exceptional Italian eatery delights its regulars with a basic menu
of rustic pleasures: panini, a single
pasta dish and a superb plate of
mixed antipastos drizzled with
olive oil. The shelves are stacked
with wine, the coffee is perfect and
the desserts are sinfully good.

🍽 ELY *Modern Irish* €€€

☎ 676 8986; www.elywinebar.ie; 22 Ely
Pl; 🕙 noon-3pm Mon-Fri, 1-4pm Sat,
6-9.30pm Mon-Wed, to 10.30pm Thu-Sat;
🚍 10, 15

Scrummy burgers, bangers and
mash or wild smoked salmon salad
are some of what you'll find in this
basement restaurant. Dishes are
prepared with organic and free-
range produce from the owner's
family farm in County Clare, so
you can be assured of the quality.
There's a large wine list to choose
from, with more than 70 by the
glass. There is also a new branch of
Ely in the old tobacco warehouse
in Customs House Quay.

🍽 L'ECRIVAIN *French* €€€

☎ 661 1919; www.lecrivain.com; 112
Lower Baggot St; 🕙 12.30-2pm Mon-Fri,
7-11pm Mon-Sat; 🚍 10, 11, 13b, 51

Two nods from Messrs Michelin
suggest that this could be the best
in town – and many foodies agree.
Combinations of the freshest local,
seasonal produce – wild salmon,
Dublin Bay prawns, veal and
Barbary duck – are matched with
inventive sauces and accompani-
ments and presented like works of
art. Has an attentive, friendly staff.

🍽 RESTAURANT PATRICK
GUILBAUD *French* €€€

☎ 676 4192; www.restaurantpatrick
guilbaud.ie; 21 Upper Merrion St;
🕙 12.30-2.15pm & 7.30-10.15pm Tue-
Sat; 🚍 all city-centre

The *other* contender for best in the
city also boasts two Michelin stars

Ready for service at Restaurant Patrick Guilbaud

for the French *campagnard* cuisine from Guillaume Lebrun's kitchen and the formal and faultless service that makes dining here a near perfect experience. Surprisingly, the dishes are not overly fussy; it's just excellent produce, beautifully cooked and well presented.

🍴 SHANAHAN'S ON THE GREEN *Steakhouse* €€€
☎ 407 0939; www.shanahans.ie; 119 W St Stephen's Green; 🕙 closed lunch Mon-Thu, Sat & Sun; 🚍 all city-centre, 🚊 St Stephen's Green; ♿

'American-style steakhouse' hardly does justice to this elegant restaurant, where JR Ewing and his cronies would happily have done business. Although the menu features seafood, this place is all about meat, notably the best cuts of impossibly juicy and tender Irish Angus beef you'll find anywhere on the island. The mountainous onion rings are the perfect accompaniment, while the sommeliers are among the best in the business.

🍴 TOWN BAR & GRILL *Modern European* €€€
☎ 662 4724; www.townbarandgrill.com; 21 Kildare St; 🕙 noon-11pm, to 10pm Sun; 🚍 10, 11, 15, 🚊 St Stephen's Green

Whatever stuffiness there is in this elegant, low-ceilinged basement restaurant is swept aside by the simply mouth-watering food,

which ranges from lamb's liver to slow-rotated rabbit or sweet pepper–stuffed lamb. It's how food should be eaten.

🍴 UNICORN *Italian* €€€
☎ 676 2182; 12b Merrion Ct, Merrion Row; 🕙 12.30-3.30pm & 6-11.30pm Mon-Sat; 🚍 10, 11, 13b, 51x; Ⓥ

Saturday lunch at the fashionable Unicorn has been a noisy Dublin tradition for over half a century, as media types, politicos and legal eagles gossip and clink glasses in conspiratorial rapture. At lunch many opt for the antipasto bar, but we prefer the meaty a la carte menu.

🍸 DRINK

🍸 DOHENY & NESBITT'S *Pub*
☎ 676 2945; 5 Lower Baggot St; 🚍 10, 11, 13b, 51x

Opened in 1867 as a grocer's shop, this pub has antique snugs, dark-wood panelling and a pressed-metal roof. It's a favourite haunt of politicians and journalists, with Leinster House (p55) just a short stroll away.

🍸 O'DONOGHUE'S *Pub*
☎ 676 2807; 15 Merrion Row; 🚍 10, 11, 13b, 51x

O'Donoghue's is the most renowned traditional music bar in Dublin, where well-known folk group the Dubliners started out

THE ROUNDS SYSTEM

It's said that it's impossible for two people to go to a pub for one drink, because the bedrock of Irish pub culture is the rounds system – the simple custom where someone buys you a drink and you buy one back, preferably just as the first person is finishing their drink (not you yours). Nothing will hasten your fall from social grace here like the failure to uphold this pub law.

in the 1960s. On warm summer evenings a young, international crowd spills into the courtyard beside the pub.

ⓨ TONER'S *Pub*
☎ 676 3090; 139 Lower Baggot St; 🚌 10, 11, 13b, 51x

With its stone floor and old grocer's shelves and drawers, Toner's feels like a country pub in the heart of the city. Though Victorian, it's not elaborate and draws a crowd of mainly businessmen and hacks. It's not touristy, but many visitors seek out its simple charms.

⭐ PLAY
⭐ NATIONAL CONCERT HALL
Performances
☎ bookings 417 0000, info 417 0077; www.nch.ie; Earlsfort Tce; 🕑 box office 10am-7pm Mon-Sat; 🚌 10, 11, 13, 14, 15, 44, 86, 🚋 Harcourt

Ireland's premier classical concert venue hosts performances by the National Symphony Orchestra and international artists, as well as jazz, traditional Irish and contemporary concerts. From June to September it has inexpensive concerts on Tuesday from 1.05pm to 2pm, and during the summer months it runs special concerts for kids.

⭐ RENARD'S *Club*
☎ 677 5876; www.renards.ie; S Frederick St; admission free-€10; 🕑 10.30pm-2.30am; 🚌 all city-centre

Run by Colin Farrell's godfather, and Colin's (and other celebs') favourite den of iniquity when in town, Renard's is an intimate club with a strict door policy when busy. Music is mainly house, with soul, funk and jazz making the odd appearance.

⭐ SUGAR CLUB
Club & Live Music
☎ 678 7188; www.thesugarclub.com; 8 Lower Leeson St; admission €8-20; 🕑 from 8pm; 🚌 11, 46, 118

Sink into big banquette seats with a cocktail served on the spot as you absorb up-and-coming jazz, folk, rock, indie and comedy acts in one of Dublin's most comfortable and stylish venues.

>TEMPLE BAR

There's been many a wild night had within the cobbled precincts of Temple Bar, Dublin's most visited neighbourhood, a maze of cobbled streets and alleys sandwiched between Dame St and the Liffey, running from Trinity College to Christ Church Cathedral. It has long been labelled the 'Cultural Quarter', and while there is plenty of it about, the title is hardly deserved and worn with ill-concealed discomfort. It's the inevitable consequence of an overbearing effort to sell at all costs that unquantifiable thing that is the 'Dublin Experience', as if the combination of African head masks made in China and jaded traditional music is the embodiment of Dublin's multicultural and global identity.

But it's not all booze, tack and infamy: you can browse for vintage clothes, check out the latest art installations, get your nipples pierced and nibble on Mongolian barbecue. In good weather you can watch outdoor movies in one square or join in a pulsating drum circle in another – just a few slices of life in Dublin's famed tourist district.

TEMPLE BAR

◉ SEE
City Hall 1 B3
Contemporary Music
    Centre 2 A3
Cultivate 3 B3
Gallery of Photography ... 4 C3
National Photographic
    Archive 5 C2
Original Print Gallery 6 D2
Sunlight Chambers 7 B2
Temple Bar Gallery &
    Studios 8 D2

◻ SHOP
5 Scarlet Row 9 B3
Claddagh Records 10 D2
Cow's Lane Designer
    Mart 11 B3
Flip 12 D3

Forbidden Planet 13 E2
Haus 14 D3
Retrospect 15 B3
Temple Bar Farmers
    Market 16 C2
Urban Outfitters 17 D2

◫ EAT
Chameleon 18 D2
Eden 19 C2
Elephant & Castle 20 E2
Gruel 21 C3
Larder 22 B3
Mermaid Café 23 C3
Monty's of Kathmandu .. 24 D3
Queen of Tarts 25 B3
Queen of Tarts 26 B3
Tea Room 27 C2
Zaytoon 28 B2

▼ DRINK
Octagon Bar 29 C2
Oliver St John
    Gogarty's 30 E2
Palace Bar 31 F2
Porterhouse Brewing
    Company 32 B2

★ PLAY
Button Factory 33 D2
Ha'penny Bridge Inn 34 D2
Irish Film Institute 35 D3
Mezz 36 D3
Olympia Theatre 37 C3
Project Arts Centre 38 C2
Think Tank 39 D3

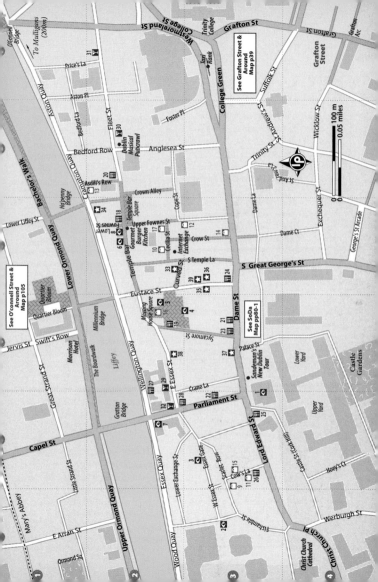

◉ SEE

◉ CITY HALL

☎ 222 2204; www.dublincity.ie; Cork Hill; admission €4/2; ☽ 10am-5.15pm Mon-Sat, 11am-5pm Sun; 🚌 50, 50a, 54, 56a, 77, 77a, 123, 150

Restored to its Georgian glory, Dublin's City Hall is adorned with neoclassical columns, a domed, gilded rotunda and patterned marble floors. Built by Thomas Cooley as the Royal Exchange from 1769 to 1779, the funerals of Michael Collins and Charles Stewart Parnell were held here. The *Story of the Capital* exhibition in the arched vaults traces Dublin's history with interesting artefacts, models and multimedia displays.

HANDEL WITH CARE

In 1742 the nearly broke GF Handel conducted the very first performance of his epic work *Messiah* in the since-demolished Dublin Music Hall, on the city's oldest street, Fishamble St. Ironically, Jonathan Swift – author of *Gulliver's Travels* and dean of St Patrick's Cathedral – having suggested his own and Christchurch's choir participate, revoked his invitation, vowing to 'punish such vicars for their rebellion, disobedience and perfidy'. The concert went ahead nonetheless, and the celebrated work is now performed at the original spot in Dublin annually.

◉ CONTEMPORARY MUSIC CENTRE

☎ 490 1857; www.cmc.ie; 19 Fishamble St; admission free; ☽ 10am-5.30pm Mon-Fri; 🚌 all city-centre

Anyone with an interest in Irish contemporary music must visit the CMC's national archive where you can hear (and play around with on an electronic organ) 5000 samples from composers of this and the last century. There's also a good reference library where you can attend courses and meet composers.

◉ CULTIVATE

☎ 674 5773; www.sustainable.ie; 15-19 W Essex St; admission free; ☽ 10am-5.30pm Mon-Sat; 🚌 all city-centre

Dublin's sustainable living centre is a one-stop shop for all you ever wanted to know about eco-living. As well as selling everything from electric bikes to wood-pellet stoves, it organises workshops and slow food brunches.

◉ GALLERY OF PHOTOGRAPHY

☎ 671 4654; www.galleryofphotography.ie; Meeting House Sq; admission free; ☽ 11am-6pm Tue-Sat, from 1pm Sun; 🚌 all city-centre

Ireland's premier photographic gallery, this place has ever-changing exhibits, often with Irish themes, including photographs of

Dublin in the 'rare auld times,' as per the popular Dublin ditty.

🎦 NATIONAL PHOTOGRAPHIC ARCHIVE

☎ 603 0371; www.nli.ie; admission free; ⏰ 10am-5pm Mon-Fri, to 2pm Sat; 🚌 all city-centre

Directly across the square from the Gallery of Photography you'll find this archive, which displays predominantly historical photographs from the National Library's collection.

🎦 ORIGINAL PRINT GALLERY

☎ 677 3657; www.originalprint.ie; 4 Temple Bar; admission free; ⏰ 10.30am-5.30pm Mon-Fri, 11am-5pm Sat, 2-6pm Sun; 🚌 all city-centre, 🚆 Jervis

The gallery's back catalogue of work from 150 Irish and international printmakers is available for purchase, along with new, limited-edition work. It's a great place to browse for pressies (yes, for yourself, too) – many starting at under €100 – among the diverse range of prints on display.

🎦 SUNLIGHT CHAMBERS

Essex Quay; 🚌 all city-centre

On the southern banks of the Liffey, Sunlight Chambers stands out among the Georgian and modern architecture for its beautiful art nouveau frieze-work. Sunlight was a brand of soap made by Lever Brothers. The frieze shows the Lever Brothers' view of the world: men make clothes dirty, women wash them.

🎦 TEMPLE BAR GALLERY & STUDIOS

☎ 671 0073; www.templebargallery .com; 5-9 Temple Bar; ⏰ 11am-6pm Tue, Wed, Fri & Sat, to 7pm Thu; 🚌 all city-centre, 🚆 Jervis

TBG has contemporary, thoughtful exhibits in a variety of media from a broad range of local and

Hustle and bustle in a Temple Bar lane

international artists. Set up in 1983 as an artist-run space, the gallery provides affordable studios and presents interesting shows from emerging painters, sculptors and mixed-media artists.

🛍 SHOP

🏠 5 SCARLET ROW *Clothing*
☎ 672 9534; 5 Scarlet Row, W Essex St; 🕐 11am-6pm Mon-Sat; 🚇 all city-centre
Beautiful, modern, exclusive, minimalist. If that's what you're after try the creations of Eley Kishimoto, Zero, Irish designer Sharon Wauchob or menswear label Unis. Owner Eileen Shields worked with Donna Karan in New York before founding her own gorgeous shoe label that retails here.

🏠 CLADDAGH RECORDS *Music*
☎ 677 0262; 2 Cecilia St; 🕐 10.30am-5.30pm Mon-Fri, from noon Sat; 🚇 all city-centre, 🚉 Jervis
The best shop in town for all your folk, traditional and ethnic musical needs. Claddagh's friendly and knowledgeable staff will guide you through the best music from Ireland, the USA and South America.

🏠 COW'S LANE DESIGNER MART *Clothing & Accessories*
Cow's Lane; 🕐 10am-5pm Sat; 🚇 all city-centre
A real hipsters' market, this Saturday collective brings together

more than 60 of the best clothing, accessory and craft stalls in town. Buy punky T-shirts, retro handbags and cutting-edge designer duds, not to mention wool spun right in front of you and creations from Ireland's only bone jeweller.

🏠 FLIP *Men's Clothing*
☎ 671 4299; 4 Fownes St; 🕐 10am-6pm Mon-Wed & Fri, to 7pm Thu & Sat, 1.30-6pm Sun; 🚇 all city-centre, 🚉 Jervis
This hip Irish label takes the best male fashion moods of the 1950s and serves them back to us, minus the mothball smell. US college shirts, logo T-shirts, Oriental and Hawaiian shirts, Fonz-style leather jackets and well-cut jeans mix it with the genuine secondhand gear upstairs.

🏠 FORBIDDEN PLANET *Books*
☎ 671 0688; 5-6 Crampton Quay; 🕐 10am-7pm Mon-Wed & Fri, to 8pm Thu, to 6pm Sat, 11am-4pm Sun; 🚇 all city-centre, 🚉 Abbey St
Science-fiction and fantasy specialist, with books, videos, comics, magazines, figurines and posters. Just the place for those Dr Spock ears or a *Star Wars* light sabre.

🏠 HAUS *Home Decor*
☎ 679 5155; 3-4 Crow St; 🕐 9am-6pm Mon-Fri, from 10am Sat; 🚇 all city-centre

Cutting-edge designer furniture and home wares from the drawing boards of the big names, such as Phillipe Starck, Le Corbusier and Ireland's own Eileen Gray.

RETROSPECT *Home Decor*

☎ 672 6188; 2 Cow's Lane; ⏲ 11.30am-6.30pm Mon, Fri & Sat, to 5pm Wed, to 7pm Thu, 11am-4pm Sun; 🚌 all city-centre

All you children of the 1960s and '70s can relive the era that taste forgot (or took off, depending on your viewpoint) at this vintage interiors shop. In here you'll discover fantastic plastic objects of desire, Formica-top tables, original lava lamps and swinging egg seats, all of them in glorious technicolour.

TEMPLE BAR FARMERS MARKET *Market*

Meeting House Sq; ⏲ 9am-4.30pm Sat; 🚌 all city-centre, 🚇 Jervis

This little market is a fabulous place to while away a Saturday morning, sampling the organic gourmet goodies bound by the market's one rule: local producers only. From cured meats to wild flowers, you could fill an entire pantry with its selection of delights.

URBAN OUTFITTERS *Clothing & Home Decor*

☎ 670 6202; 7 Fownes St; ⏲ 10am-7pm Mon-Wed & Fri, to 8pm Thu & Sat, 11am-6pm Sun; 🚌 all city-centre

Funky street wear and labels are mixed with gadgets and home

Tempting treats on display at the Temple Bar Farmers Market

wares at this branch of the US chain. As the DJ spins tunes from the Carbon record outlet, boys browse through G-Star denims, Pringle knits and Fiorucci trousers, while girls have a choice between Claudie Pierlot, W&LT and Mandarina Duck.

🍴 EAT

🍴 CHAMELEON *Indonesian* €

☎ 671 0362; www.chameleonrestaurant
.com; 1 Lower Fownes St; 🕙 6-11pm
Tue-Sat, to 10pm Sun; 🚍 all city-centre;
♿ Ⓥ

Friendly, characterful and draped in exotic fabrics, Chameleon serves up oodles of noodles and Indonesian classics such as satay, *gado gado* (veggies with peanut sauce), *nasi goreng* (fried rice) and *mee goreng* (spicy fried noodles). If you simply cannot make up your mind, try the *rijsttafel* – a selection of several dishes served with rice.

🍴 EDEN *Modern Irish* €€

☎ 670 5372; www.edenrestaurant
.ie; Meeting House Sq; 🕙 noon-3pm &
6-10.30pm, to 11pm Sat & Sun;
🚍 all city-centre; ♿ Ⓥ

Reminiscent of a swimming pool, with its aquamarine mosaic walls and ceiling-to-floor windows onto Meeting House Sq, Eden's minimalist surroundings belie the organic seasonal menu that brings the best of Irish produce to your

Cool creams predominate in Eden restaurant

table. Castletownbere scallops with sautéed potatoes and the pan-fried fillet of Irish beef are clear winners with its glitteringly hip patrons.

🍴 ELEPHANT & CASTLE

Diner €€

☎ 679 3121; www.elephantandcastle
.ie; 18 Temple Bar; 🕙 8am-11.30pm
Mon-Fri, 11.30am-11.30pm Sat & Sun;
🚍 all city-centre; ♿ Ⓥ

If it's massive New York–style sandwiches or sticky chicken wings you're after, this bustling upmarket diner is just the joint. Be prepared to queue though, especially at weekends when Elephant & Castle heaves with the hassled parents of wandering toddlers, wealthy suburbanites and hung-over 20-somethings, all in pursuit of a carb-fest and quiet corner to peruse the paper.

🍴 GRUEL *Modern European* €
☎ 670 7119; 68a Dame St; 🕒 7am-9.30pm Mon-Fri, 10.30am-4pm Sat & Sun; 🚌 all city-centre; Ⓥ

For its regulars, Gruel is the best dish in town, whether for the super-filling, tasty lunchtime roast-in-a-roll – a rotating list of slow-roasted organic meats stuffed into a bap and flavoured with homemade relishes – or the exceptional evening menu, where pasta, fish and chicken are given an exotic once-over. Go, queue, and share elbow space with the table behind you: it's worth the effort. Bookings not accepted.

🍴 LARDER *Cafe* €
☎ 633 3581; 8 Parliament St; 🕒 7.30am-5.30pm Mon-Fri, from 9am Sat; 🚌 7b, 11, 121; 🚻 Ⓥ

This warm and welcoming cafe-restaurant has an organic vibe to it, what with its wholesome porridge breakfasts, gourmet sandwiches – such as serrano ham, gruyere and rocket – and Japanese speciality *suki* teas (try the China gunpowder). It's confident about its food – we like the fact that it lists suppliers – and so are we.

🍴 MERMAID CAFÉ
Modern European €€€
☎ 670 8236; www.mermaid.ie; 69 Dame St; 🕒 12.30-2.30pm & 6-11pm Mon-Sat, 12.30-3pm & 6-9pm Sun; 🚌 all city-centre; 🚻 Ⓥ

This French-American style bistro with elemental furniture and sparse artwork on its walls caters to a hip gourmand crowd who appreciate inventive ingredient-led, organic food such as robust cassoulets, New England crab cakes or mouth-watering steaks.

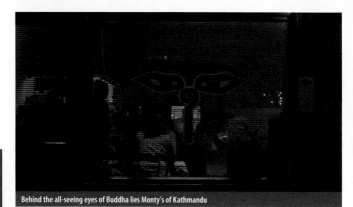
Behind the all-seeing eyes of Buddha lies Monty's of Kathmandu

The informal atmosphere, friendly staff and pure food often make it difficult to get a table without a prior reservation.

🍴 MONTY'S OF KATHMANDU
Nepalese €€
☎ 670 4911; www.montys.ie; 28 Eustace St; 🕙 12.30-2.30pm & 6-11.30pm Mon-Sat, 6-11pm Sun; 🚍 all city-centre; Ⓥ

The daily trade of the award-winning Monty's is built on people who keep returning for typical Nepalese dishes such as *gorkhali* (chicken cooked in chilli, yoghurt and ginger) or *kachila* (raw marinated meat). The Shiva beer complements these hearty, spicy dishes. Its convenient location opposite the Irish Film Institute (p75) makes it good for a post-movie bite.

🍴 QUEEN OF TARTS
Bakery & Cafe €
☎ 670 7499; Cork Hill; 🕙 7.30am-6pm Mon-Fri, from 9am Sat, from 10am Sun; 🚍 all city-centre; 🕭

Pocket-sized Queen of Tarts was so popular with its wide array of mouth-watering savoury tarts and filled focaccias, fruit crumbles and wicked pastries, that they opened a bigger version around the corner on Cow's Lane. Either is perfect for breakfast or lunch.

🍴 TEA ROOM
French & Modern Irish €€€
☎ 407 0813; www.theclarence.ie; Clarence, 6-8 Wellington Quay; 🕙 7-10.30pm Tue-Sat; 🚍 all city-centre

A high-vaulted ceiling with tall, elegant windows and handsome wood panelling makes the Tea Room a veritable cathedral to haute cuisine, and looks do not deceive. Guided by the expert hand of chef Mathieu Melin, the ambitious menu features classic French cuisine – based equally on fish and meat – with a serious Irish twist. Think Irish spring lamb with sweetbreads or seabass with a grapegruit and coriander sauce. It's well-prepared, beautifully presented seasonal food that is definitely a pleasure to eat.

🍴 ZAYTOON *Middle Eastern* €

☎ 677 3595; 14-15 Parliament St; ⏰ noon-4am; 🚌 all city-centre

Fast food without the guilt? Absorb the booze with a late-night stop at the city's best kebab joint, the best place to feed the munchies on the way to bed.

🍸 DRINK

🍸 MULLIGANS *Pub*

☎ 677 5582; 8 Poolbeg St; 🚌 14, 44, 47, 48, 62, 🚆 Tara St

Outside the northeastern boundary of Temple Bar, Mulligans has scarcely changed over the years. It featured as the local in the film *My Left Foot* and is also popular with journalists from the nearby newspaper offices. Mulligan's was established in 1782 and has long been reputed to have the best Guinness in Ireland, as well as a wonderfully varied collection of regulars.

🍸 OCTAGON BAR *Bar*

☎ 670 9000; Clarence, 6-8 Wellington Quay; 🚌 all city-centre

This swish bar at the Clarence, owned by U2, has an odd atmosphere not helped by the artificial daylight and anodyne music

MICRO-REVOLUTION

A number of Dublin microbreweries are challenging the supremacy of Guinness. One is **Messrs Maguire** (Map p105, D4; ☎ 670 5777; www.messrsmaguire.ie; 1-2 Burgh Quay), a gigantic 'uberbar' spread across three levels that offers five of its own brews, from a creamy porter to the German-style Haus beer. Another is the **Dublin Brewing Company** (Map p105, A3; ☎ 872 8622; www.simtec.us/dublinbrewing; 141 N King St; ⏰ 9am-5.30pm Mon-Fri), which sells its four beers, including the well-loved brew Revolution Red, during business hours only.

The best known, however, is the **Porterhouse Brewing Company** (☎ 679 8847; www .porterhousebrewco.com; 16-18 Parliament St) in Temple Bar. Porterhouse is the brainchild of cousins Oliver Hughes and Liam Lahart who, in 1989, spotted a gap in the market for locally brewed beers. They soon learned not to underestimate Dubliner's thirst for a decent pint. From humble beginnings in their small Temple Bar brewery they expanded and now bring their 10 delicious beers (including the award-winning Oyster stout) to appreciative swillers all across Ireland and the UK.

policy. It's probably the only place in Temple Bar, though, where you'll find 30-something Dubliners or the odd resident celebrity having a quiet G&T.

▼ OLIVER ST JOHN GOGARTY'S *Trad Music Pub*
☎ 671 1822; 58-59 Fleet St; ✦ sessions 2.30-7pm & 9pm-2am Mon-Sat, noon-2pm, 5-7pm & 8.30pm-1am Sun; ▣ all city-centre

It mightn't be the most authentic trad session in town, but it's no less enjoyable and the musicians who keep the tourists entertained can certainly play a bit. Come early to get a seat.

▼ PALACE BAR *Pub*
☎ 677 9290; 21 Fleet St; ▣ all city-centre
With its mirrors, etched glass and wooden niches, Palace Bar is often said to be the perfect example

The eponymous poet of the Oliver St John Gogarty's Pub

of an old Dublin pub. It's popular with journalists from the nearby *Irish Times* and was patronised by writers Patrick Kavanagh and Flann O'Brien last century.

PLAY

⭐ BUTTON FACTORY
Club & Live Music

☎ 670 9202; www.buttonfactory.ie; Curved St; 🕙 from 7.30pm nightly, clubs 11.30pm-3.30am Thu-Sun; 🚇 all city-centre

A top-class sound system, a big main stage, a proper dance pit and a carpeted back bar are the ingredients that make this a contender for best venue in town, for both live music and DJ gigs. From punk to dancehall, from alt rock to electro, there's something for every taste. Show up for the live gig and stay for the club. Saturday night's Transmission (electro, dance) is especially recommended.

⭐ HA'PENNY BRIDGE INN
Comedy

☎ 677 0616; 42 Wellington Quay; admission €10/8; 🕙 shows start 9pm Tue-Thu; 🚇 all city-centre

From Tuesday through Thursday you can hear some pretty funny comedians (and some truly awful ones) do their shtick in the upstairs room of this Temple Bar institution, which has remained unchanged since the '70s. Tuesday night's

Battle of the Axe, an improv night that features a great deal of crowd participation, is the best.

⭐ IRISH FILM INSTITUTE (IFI)
Cinema

☎ 679 5744; www.irishfilm.ie; 6 Eustace St; matinees/evenings €7.50/8; 🕙 centre 10am-11.30pm, films 2-11pm; 🚇 all city-centre

The IFI shows classics and new independent flicks. You have to be a member to see a movie, but you can buy a one-week membership with your ticket for €1 per group. It has mother-and-baby screenings and the complex also has a bar, cafe and excellent bookshop.

⭐ MEZZ *Live Music*

☎ 670 7655; 23-24 Eustace St; admission free-€20; 🕙 to 2.30am Mon-Sat, to 11pm Sun; 🚇 all city-centre

Dark, sweaty and loud: it's the way music venues used to be in those heady days before standard lamps and leather sofas became, well, standard. Old-school rock, electronic, funk and garage bands belt it out most nights to a young up-for-it crowd.

⭐ OLYMPIA THEATRE
Live music & Performances

☎ 677 7744; 72 Dame St; 🕙 box office 10am-6.30pm Mon-Sat; 🚇 all city-centre

This is an ornate old Victorian music hall that specialises in light

 Arveene Juthan
One of Ireland's best-known dance DJs, a regular guest of The Prodigy and Soulwax

The Dublin scene Dublin doesn't do full-on raves, but it has a great culture of parties hosted by smaller clubs and venues. **Essence of a good night out** Everyone should be on the level; even if people don't know you they treat you like they do. **Best night out** Sunday in Ukiyo (p91), where you can hear the likes of Jason O'Callaghan throw down some serious disco. Another great venue with the same kind of ethos is Twisted Pepper (p119). **Favourite club nights** My choices would be Transmission on a Saturday night in the Button Factory (p75) or Antics on a Wednesday night in the PoD (p94), both of which are popular with a new generation of clubber, whose musical tastes are pretty sophisticated thanks to the influence of travel and the internet.

plays, comedy and, around Christmas time, panto. In recent years though, pleasantly tatty Olympia Theatre has gained more of a reputation for the live gigs it hosts, which have included performances by some big international acts.

⭐ PROJECT ARTS CENTRE
Performances
☎ 881 9613; www.project.ie; 39 E Essex St; 🕙 box office 11am-7pm Mon-Sat; 🚌 all city-centre

The Project Arts Centre's three stages (including a black box) are home to experimental plays from up-and-coming Irish and foreign writers. Some are brilliant, others execrable, but there's excitement in taking risks.

⭐ THINK TANK *Club*
☎ 635 9991; www.thethinktank.ie; 24 Eustace St; admission €6-15; 🕙 8pm-late; 🚌 all city-centre

Dance DJs, Battle of the Bands nights, visiting live acts and nu-

Stark blue facade of the Project Arts Centre

merous other assorted festivities make up the menu at this basement club in Temple Bar – Strictly Handbag, Dublin's longest running club night, takes place on Monday nights and still draws them in with its fun mixed bag of '80s tunes.

>SODA

It's a made-up name (by us, thank you very much) but it refers to a very real and very distinctive neighbourhood – the stretch of streets that runs *South of Dame St* from Grafton St's western edge right to the eastern boundary of the Liberties. You'll find the city at its funkiest here, from the independently owned boutiques to the supercool bars and clubs that give the area its boho flavour. In fact, SoDa is making 'alternative' a personality. It's here you'll find Dublin's single best attraction in the Chester Beatty Library, plus groovy markets, alternative shops, atmospheric old pubs and the best ethnic eats in town. From superstylin' S William St to convivial Camden St, SoDa is Dublin's anarchic heart.

SODA

◉ SEE
Chester Beatty Library ...**1** B2
Dublin Castle **2** B2
Shaw Birthplace **3** C8
Whitefriar Street
 Carmelite Church **4** C4

🛍 SHOP
A Store is Born **5** D3
Asia Food Market **6** C3
Barry Doyle Design
 Jewellers **7** C2
Caru **8** D2
Coppinger Row Market ...**9** D3
Costume **10** D2
Decor **11** C5
George's Street Arcade ...**12** C2
Harlequin ....(see 10)
Jenny Vander **13** D3
Low Key **14** C2
Neptune Gallery **15** D3
Neu Bleu Eriu **16** D2
Smock **17** D2
Walton's **18** C2
Wild Child **19** C2

🍴 EAT
Bar With No Name **20** C3
Blazing Salads **21** D2
Café Bar Deli **22** C2
Cake Cafe **23** C7
Coppinger Row **24** D3
Fallon & Byrne **25** D2
Good World **26** C2
Gourmet Burger
 Kitchen **27** D2
Govinda **28** C3
Green Nineteen **29** C6
Honest to Goodness ...**30** C2
Juice **31** C2
Lemon **32** D2
Leon **33** D2
L'Gueuleton **34** C3
Odessa **35** C2
Shebeen Chic **36** C2
Silk Road Cafe ....(see 1)
Simon's Place **37** C2
Ukiyo **38** C2

🍸 DRINK
Anseo **39** C6
Bar With No Name .....(see 20)
Bernard Shaw **40** C8
Bia Bar **41** C3
Dragon **42** C2
George **43** C2
Grogan's Castle
 Lounge **44** D3
Long Hall **45** C3
Market Bar **46** C3
Solas **47** C5
Stag's Head **48** C2

★ PLAY
Andrew's Lane
 Theatre **49** D2
Crawdaddy **50** D7
JJ Smyth's **51** C3
Rí Rá **52** C2
Tripod **53** D7
Village **54** C6
Whelan's **55** C6

Please see over for map

◎ SEE

◎ CHESTER BEATTY LIBRARY

☎ 407 0750; www.cbl.ie; Dublin Castle,
Cork Hill; admission free; ⏱ 10am-5pm
Mon-Fri, 11am-5pm Sat, 1-5pm Sun,
closed Mon Oct-Apr, free tours 1pm Wed,
3pm & 4pm Sun; 🚌 50, 51b, 77, 78a,
123; ♿

The astounding collection of New
York mining magnate Sir Alfred
Chester Beatty (1875–1968) is the
basis for not just one of Dublin's
best museums, but one of the
finest of its kind to be found
anywhere in the world. Inside
you'll find manuscripts, miniature
paintings, books, bindings and
calligraphies – including maybe

> **JUSTICE FOR ALL?**
> The Figure of Justice that faces Dublin
> Castle's Upper Yard from the Cork Hill
> entrance has a controversial history.
> The statue was seen as a snub by many
> Dubliners, who felt Justice was sym-
> bolically turning her back on the city.
> If that wasn't enough, when it rained
> the scales would fill with water and
> tilt, rather than remaining perfectly
> balanced. Eventually a hole was drilled
> in the bottom of each pan, restoring
> balance, sort of.

the West's most stunning collection of Korans – and the world's
second-oldest biblical fragment.
See also p16.

◎ DUBLIN CASTLE

☎ 677 7129; www.dublincastle.ie;
Cork Hill, Dame St; admission €4.50/3;
⏱ 10am-4.45pm Mon-Fri, from 2pm Sat;
🚌 50, 54, 56a, 77, 77a

The stronghold of British power
in Ireland for 700 years, Dublin
Castle is mostly an 18th-century
creation built on Norman and
Viking foundations. Of the 13th-
century Anglo-Norman fortress
built on the site, only the record
tower remains. Once the official
residence of the British viceroys in
Ireland and now used by the Irish
Government, a tour will appeal to
history and architecture buffs. On
Sunday and holidays free tours
run every 30 minutes. Please note

Relax in the gardens at the Chester Beatty Library

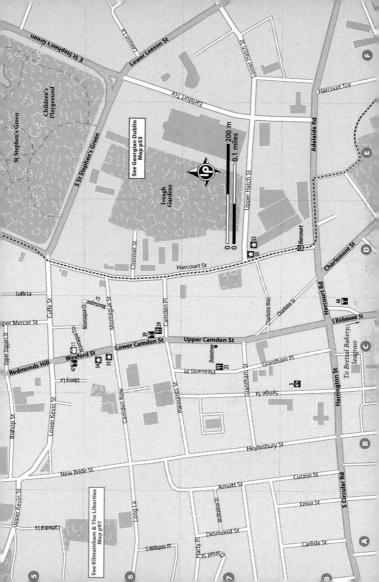

E St Stephen's Green

Lower Leeson St

Lesson Cross

Earlsfort Tce

Lower Hatch St

Harcourt Tce

Children's Playground

St Stephen's Green

N St Stephen's Green

See Georgian Dublin
Map p53

Iveagh Gardens

Adelaide Rd

200 m
0.1 miles

Upper Hatch St

Charlemont St

50
53

Harcourt

Harcourt Rd

Harcourt St

Cuffe La

Cuffe St

Montague Ct

Montague La

Camden Pl

Charlotte Way

Charlotte St

Charlemont Rd

40

S Richmond St

Montague St

Upper Mercer St

Upper Digges St

Montague La

Wexford St

39

29

Lower Camden St

Upper Camden St

Harrington St

To Bretzel Bakery;
Seagrass

Redmonds Hill

47

54

55

Daintree

17

23

Grantham St

Grantham Pl

Bishop St

Lower Kevin St

Liberty La

Camden Row

Pleasants Pl

Pleasants St

Grantham St

Synge St

Upper Kevin St

Cathedral La

New Bride St

Long La

Heytesbury St

S Circular Rd

See Kilmainham & The Liberties
Map p97

S Williams Pl

Harty Pl

Daniel St

Arnott St

Malland St

Desmond St

Curzon St

Emor St

Carlisle St

A

B

C

D

E

F

5

6

7

8

that the State Apartments may be closed at short notice – call ahead to check.

SHAW BIRTHPLACE
☎ 475 0854; 33 Synge St; admission €6/5; ☽ 10am-1pm & 2-5pm Mon-Sat, plus 11am-1pm & 2-5pm Sun May-Sep; 🚌 16, 19, 122

Entering (through velvet drapes) the atmospheric birthplace and museum on playwright George Bernard Shaw, an unassuming house on a sleepy terrace, is like stepping back in time to middle-class Victorian Dublin. The 'time machine' audio-tour (in several languages) has a wonderfully evocative soundscape full of witty asides about Victorian social mores.

WHITEFRIAR STREET CARMELITE CHURCH
☎ 475 8821; 56 Aungier St; ☽ 8am-6.30pm Mon & Wed-Sat, to 8.30pm Tue, to 7.30pm Sun; 🚌 16, 16a, 16c, 19, 19a, 65, 83

On the former site of a Carmelite monastery, this huge church houses a 16th-century Flemish oak statue of the Mother and Child, thought to be the only one of its kind to survive the Reformation. The altar contains the remains of St Valentine, donated by Pope Gregory XVI in 1835.

🛍 SHOP
🛍 A STORE IS BORN
Clothing & Accessories
☎ 679 5866; 34 Clarendon St; ☽ 10am-6pm Sat; 🚇 all city-centre, 🚋 St Stephen's Green

Discreetly hidden for six days a week behind a garage roller-door, this store opens up on Saturday to reveal a bounty of paisley dresses, peasant tops, cashmere cardies, belts, beads, sequined singlets, wide-collared men's shirts and suit pants.

🛍 ASIA FOOD MARKET
Gourmet Food
☎ 677 9764; 18 Drury St; ☽ 10am-7pm Mon-Sat; 🚌 16, 16a, 19, 19a, 65, 83, 🚋 St Stephen's Green

This large, friendly food emporium should be your first port of call

PASSION FOR FASHION
After years in the wilderness, Irish designers are making a name for themselves on the international stage. John Rocha, whose own-label clothes have been high fashion for the past decade, has branched into home wares (available in Brown Thomas, p42) and hotel design, as has milliner-to-the-supermodels Philip Treacy, who recently designed the flamboyant G Hotel in Galway. Other Irish names currently making a splash internationally include Joanne Hynes, Pauric Sweeney and N & C Kilkenny.

if you want to whip up an Asian feast. For a start it's really good value, and you'll find everything here from kitchen implements to hard-to-come-by ingredients such as grass jelly, habanero chillies, brown basmati rice or – should you wish – chicken's feet.

🖾 BARRY DOYLE DESIGN
JEWELLERS *Jewellery*
☎ 671 2838; George's St Arcade; 🕒 9am-6pm Mon-Wed, Fri & Sat, to 8pm Thu; 🚇 15, 16, 19, 83
Upstairs on the southern side of George's St Arcade, Barry Doyle works away in his light-filled wooden studio producing bold, beautiful, handmade necklaces, bracelets and rings in Celtic and modern designs. Individual pieces can be commissioned – prices are steep, but the work is of excellent quality.

🖾 CARU *Clothing*
☎ 613 9000; 30 Drury St; 🕒 10.30am-6pm Mon-Fri, 10am-6pm Sat; 🚇 all city-centre
From European shabby chic to New York high fashion and LA casual trendy, labels including Alice + Olivia, Diabless, Julia Clancey, Suzie Wong, Felix Rey and Hudson Jeans are on the racks here and on the backs of Angelina Jolie, Sienna Miller and Jennifer Aniston.

🖾 COPPINGER ROW MARKET
Gourmet Food
☎ 222 3377; Coppinger Row; 🕒 9am-7pm Thu; 🚇 all city-centre
This weekly market keeps the focus on small artisan food growers from around the country, who gather here to sell their delicious goodies and address the curiosity of their customers. There's sandwiches, crepes and cheeses to go, plus a fine selection of fruit and veg and other organic fare.

🖾 COSTUME *Women's Clothing*
☎ 679 4188; 10 Castle Market; 🕒 10am-6pm Mon-Wed, Fri & Sat, to 7pm Thu, noon-5pm Sun; 🚇 all city-centre, 🚉 St Stephen's Green
From casuals to sparkly full-length dresses, Costume specialises in stylish contemporary women's wear from young European designers. Its own Costume label sits alongside pieces by Isabel Marant, Anna Sui, Jonathan Saunders and Irish label Leighlee.

🖾 DECOR *Home Decor*
☎ 475 9010; 14a Wexford St; 🕒 10am-6pm Mon-Sat; 🚇 16, 16a, 16c, 19, 19a, 65, 83, 🚉 St Stephen's Green
Decor is crammed with chunky teak and mahogany furniture from Southeast Asia, basalt Buddha statues, off-beat gilded mirrors and exotic throws – and all at a price we like, to boot.

☐ GEORGE'S STREET ARCADE
Books, Clothing & Gifts

☽ 10am-6pm Mon-Sat; 🚌 all city-centre
Dublin's best nonfood market
(sadly there's not much competition) is sheltered within an elegant
Victorian Gothic arcade between
S Great George's and Drury Sts.
Apart from shops and stalls selling
new and old clothes, secondhand
books, hats, posters, jewellery and
records, there's a fortune teller,
gourmet nibbles and a fish and
chipper who does a roaring trade.

☐ HARLEQUIN
Clothing & Accessories

☎ 671 0202; 13 Castle Market;
☽ 10.30am-6pm Mon-Wed, Fri & Sat,
to 7pm Thu; 🚌 all city-centre, 🚃 St
Stephen's Green
A fantastically cluttered shop, jam-
packed with authentic vintage
clothing from the 1920s onwards,
as well as satin gloves, top hats,
snakeskin bags and jet-beaded
chokers.

☐ JENNY VANDER
Clothing & Accessories

☎ 677 0406; 50 Drury St; ☽ 10am-
5.45pm Mon-Sat; 🚌 all city-centre,
🚃 St Stephen's Green
More *Breakfast at Tiffany's* than
Hair, this secondhand store oozes
elegance and sophistication.
Exquisite beaded handbags, fur-
trimmed coats, richly patterned

dresses and costume jewellery
priced as if it were the real thing
are snapped up by discerning
fashionistas and film stylists.

☐ LOW KEY *Clothing*

☎ 677 0299; 23 Georges St Arcade;
☽ 9.30am-6pm Mon-Wed, Fri & Sat, to
8pm Thu, 2-6pm Sun; 🚌 15, 16, 19, 83
Low-key boutique stocked with
oversized sweatshirts, surfy dresses and low-slung jeans for boys
and girls who prefer understated
cool to glitzy glam. Labels include
Fever, St Martin, Snob and Dollar.

☐ NEPTUNE GALLERY *Maps*

☎ 671 5021; 1st fl, 41 S William St;
☽ 10am-5.30pm Mon-Fri, 10am-1pm
Sat; 🚌 all city-centre, 🚃 St Stephen's
Green
Climb the rickety stairs over
Busyfeet Cafe into this Aladdin's
Cave of cartography. Pick up dusty
maps and prints of Ireland dating
from 1600 to 1880 for anything
from a few quid up to €1000.

☐ NEU BLUE ERIU
Body Products

☎ 672 5776; 7 S William St; ☽ 10am-
8pm Mon-Thu, to 6pm Fri & Sat; 🚌 all
city-centre
In a fantastic, otherworldly space,
Neu Blue Eriu sells top-end skin-
care, cosmetics and haircare from
Prada, Shu Uemura and Kleins,
as well as scented candles, oils

and artisan perfumes. Facials and massages are pricey but highly regarded.

◩ SMOCK

Women's Clothing & Accessories

☎ 613 9000; 31 Drury St; ◷ 10.30am-6pm Mon-Fri, 10am-6pm Sat; ▣ all city-centre

This tiny designer shop features cutting-edge international women's wear from classy 'investment labels' such as Easton Pearson, Veronique Branquinho and AF Vandevorst, as well as a small range of interesting jewellery and lingerie.

Designer-ware display in Smock

◩ WALTON'S *Music*

☎ 475 0661; 69-70 S Great George's St; ◷ 9am-6pm Mon-Sat, noon-5pm Sun; ▣ 16, 16a, 19, 19a, 65, 83

These traditional music specialists sell CDs, instruments, sheet music for Irish harp, flute and fiddle, and song books featuring tunes by Irish music greats, including the Wolfe Tones, the Fureys and the Dubliners. You can also take two-hour crash courses in the bodhrán (Irish drums) or tin whistle at its music school. God bless the staff.

◩ WILD CHILD

Clothing & Home Decor

☎ 675 9933; 24 George's St Arcade; ◷ 10am-6pm Mon-Wed, Fri & Sat, to 8pm Thu, noon-6pm Sun; ▣ 16, 16a, 16c, 19, 19a, 65, 83, ▤ St Stephen's Green

If you're in the market for top quality retro and vintage clothing from decades past – or an Eames chair or funky Melamine kitchen container – you've come to the right place. The stock is handpicked by owner Will Walsh, whose eye is unerringly spot-on.

▥ EAT
▥ BAR WITH NO NAME

Traditional English   €

☎ 675 3708; 3 Fade St; ◷ 4-9pm Mon-Sat, from 1.30pm Sun; ▣ 16, 80, 83

Old-style bar food with substance, like they used to serve in London

VEGETARIAN OPTIONS

Dublin has a surprising number of good vegetarian restaurants as well as a considerable number of regular restaurants offering a reasonable selection of things to graze on. The following vegetarian restaurants also have vegan dishes:

> Blazing Salads (☎ 671 9552; 42 Drury St; ☯ 10am-6pm Mon-Sat, to 8pm Thu) Excellent salad bar and sandwiches, but no seating.

> Café Fresh (Map p39, C3; ☎ 671 9669; Powerscourt Centre; ☯ 9.30am-6pm Mon-Sat, 10am-5pm Sun) Hot meals, smoothies, juices, soups and great salads.

> Cornucopia (Map p39, C2; ☎ 677 7583; 19 Wicklow St; ☯ 9am-7pm Mon-Wed, Fri & Sat, to 9pm Thu) Old-school country-kitchen-style restaurant with hearty hot dishes and brekkies.

> Govinda (☎ 475 0309; 4 Aungier St; ☯ noon-9pm) Run by Hare Krishnas, with Eastern hot meals and salads.

> Juice (☎ 475 7856; 73-83 S Great George's St; ☯ noon-10pm Mon-Thu, noon-11pm Fri & Sat, 10am-10pm Sun) Hip Pacific-rim fare and organic wines.

taverns – deep-fried whitebait, Welsh rarebit, pork rillettes and *moules frites* – is the latest venture of DJ-chef Billy Scurry, now found in the kitchen of Dublin's trendiest watering hole.

🍴 BRETZEL BAKERY *Bakery* €
☎ 475 2724; 1a Lennox St; ☯ 8.30am-3pm Mon, to 6pm Tue, Wed & Fri, to 7pm Thu, 9am-5pm Sat, 9am-1pm Sun; 🚌 14, 15, 65, 83

The bagels might be a bit on the chewy side, but they've got their charms – as do the scrumptious selections of breads, savoury snacks, cakes and biscuits that have locals queuing out the door on weekends. Certified kosher since 2003, Bretzel Bakery has been on this Portobello site, at the far southern end of SoDa, since 1870.

🍴 BOTTEGA TOFFOLI
Italian €€
☎ 633 4022; 34 Castle St; ☯ 8am-4pm Tue & Wed, 8am-9pm Thu & Fri, 11am-8pm Sat, 1-8pm Sun; 🚌 all city-centre; V ☝

Tucked away in a quiet lane is this superb Italian cafe, home of one of the best sandwiches you'll eat in town: beautifully cut prosciutto, baby tomatoes and rocket salad drizzled with imported olive oil, all on homemade *piadina* bread that is just too good to be true.

🍴 CAFÉ BAR DELI *Italian* €€
☎ 677 1646; www.cafebardeli.ie; 12-13 S Great George's St; ☯ 12.30-11pm Mon-Sat, 2-10pm Sun; 🚌 15, 16, 19, 83; V ☝

Two other branches, one on Grafton St (Map p39, C3) and one

in Ranelagh Village (Map p127, B4), testify to the success of this eternally popular restaurant's simple formula: great crispy pizzas with imaginative toppings such as spicy lamb and tzatziki, fresh homemade pastas or salads such as broccoli, feta and chickpea that you'll dream about for days. All at prices that won't break the bank in a buzzing atmosphere. What more could you want, hey?

🍴 CAKE CAFE *Cafe* €
☎ 633 4477; www.thecakecafe.ie; Daintree Building, Pleasants Pl; 🕙 10am-6pm; 🚌 16, 19, 83; ♿
Dublin's best-kept pastry secret is this great little cafe in a tough-to-find lane just off Camden St. The easiest way in is through Daintree stationery shop (61 Camden St); out the back is the self-contained yard, which in good weather is the best spot to enjoy coffee and a homemade cake.

🍴 COPPINGER ROW
Mediterranean €€
☎ 672 9884; www.coppingerrow.com; Coppinger Row; 🕙 noon-11pm Tue-Sat, 1-8pm Sun; 🚌 all city-centre
The quiet, in-the-know hype that surrounded its opening in the summer of 2009 suggested that this eatery was on to something a little bit special. The menu – which features the likes of piri-piri

spatchcock poussin with tomato rice and an excellent pan-fried calves liver with borlotti beans, bacon and sage salad – certainly lives up to expectations, but for us it's the no-fuss, friendly service that does the trick.

🍴 FALLON & BYRNE
Food Hall €€/€€€
☎ 472 1000; www.fallonandbyrne.net; Exchequer St; 🕙 9.30am-7pm Mon-Sat, noon-6pm Sun; 🚌 18, 83; Ⓥ
Dublin's answer to New York's much-loved Dean & Deluca is this upmarket food hall, wine cellar and restaurant. The queues for the delicious deli counter are constant, while the chic buzzy brasserie upstairs hasn't failed to impress either, with long red banquettes, a diverse menu of creamy fish pie, beef carpaccio and roast turbot, and excellent service.

🍴 GOOD WORLD *Chinese* €€
☎ 677 2580; 18 S Great George's St; 🕙 12.30pm-2.30am; 🚌 18, 83; Ⓥ
A hands-down winner of our best-Chinese-restaurant competition, the Good World has two menus, but to really get the most out of this terrific spot, steer well clear of the Western menu and its unimaginative dishes. With listings in two languages, the Chinese menu is packed with dishes and delicacies that keep us coming back for more.

🍴 GOURMET BURGER KITCHEN *Burgers* €€

☎ 679 0537; www.gbkinfo.com; 14 S William St; ⏱ noon-10pm Sun-Wed, to 11pm Thu-Sat; 🚌 all city-centre; Ⓥ

Burgers are back, and they don't get any better than the ones served at the three city centre branches of this new restaurant – also located at S Anne St (Map p39, C3) and Temple Bar (Map p65, D2). The menu has a range of choices, from your straight-up beef burger with cheese to something a little more adventurous: how about, for instance, a Kiwiburger – a beef burger topped with beetroot, egg, cheese, pineapple, salad leaves and relish? They also have decent vegetarian options.

🍴 GREEN NINETEEN *Modern Irish* €

☎ 478 9626; www.green19.ie; 19 Lower Camden St; ⏱ 10am-11pm Mon-Sat, noon-6pm Sun; 🚌 16, 19, 83; Ⓥ

The newest addition to Camden St's growing corridor of cool is this sleek restaurant that special-ises in locally sourced, organic grub…without the fancy price tag. Braised lamb chump, corned beef, pot roast chicken and the ubiquitous burger are but the meaty part of the menu that also includes salads and veggie op-tions. We love it.

🍴 HONEST TO GOODNESS *Cafe* €

☎ 677 5373; www.honesttogoodness .ie; George's St Arcade; ⏱ 9am-6pm Mon-Sat, noon-4pm Sun; 🚌 15, 16, 19, 83; Ⓥ

Wholesome sandwiches (made with freshly baked bread), tasty soups and a near-legendary Sloppy Joe, all made on the premises using ingredients sourced from local producers, have earned this lovely spot in the George's St Arcade a bevy of loyal fans who want to keep it all to themselves.

🍴 LEMON *Crêperie* €

☎ 672 9044; 66 S William St; ⏱ 8am-7.30pm Mon-Wed & Fri, to 9pm Thu, 9am-7.30pm Sat, 10am-6.30pm Sun; 🚌 all city-centre; Ⓥ

Lemon, which has a second branch in Dawson St (Map p39, D2), doesn't look like much – until you catch a whiff of those crepes. Then it's straight inside where a sweet or savoury crepe or waffle is yours at breakneck speed. Get it smoth-ered in sinful ice cream, chocolate sauce, coconut or Grand Marnier.

🍴 LEON *French* €€

☎ 670 7238; 33 Exchequer St; ⏱ 8am-11pm Mon-Sat, 9am-10pm Sun; 🚌 all city-centre

French elegance comes to Dublin in the shape of this cafe-restaurant. From bouillabaisse to filet of lamb

Miceal Murray
Manager of L'Gueuleton (p90)

Current Dublin dining scene There's an exciting re-interpretation of what was seen as middle-of-the-road, mid-priced casual dining. A lot of restaurants have re-imagined their menus and are offering some pretty tasty versions of standard fare. In fact, I'd say we're quite spoilt for choice! **What to look for when picking a restaurant** Consistency, friendly service and a certain amount of homeliness and familiarity. **Restaurants that fit the bill** Gruel (p71), for its kitsch decor and hearty food; Coppinger Row (p87), a buzzy, smart place that's like a local shop for locals; and Juniors (p132), which is a little off the beaten track but has well-executed standard fare.

with a gratin dauphinois, the food is classically Gallic, but the real treat here is to linger over a cappuccino with a newspaper by the open fire at the front.

🍴 L'GUEULETON *French* €€

☎ 675 3708; www.lgueuleton.com; 1 Fade St; 🕑 12.30-3pm & 6-10pm Mon-Sat; 🚍 18, 83

The name's a mouthful (it means 'the Gluttonous Feast' in French) and the no-reservations policy might test the customers' patience, but they just can't get enough of the restaurant's take on French rustic cuisine: the Toulouse sausages with *choucroute* (sauerkraut) is a reminder that when it comes to the pleasures of the palate, the French really know what they're doing.

🍴 ODESSA *Mediterranean* €€€

☎ 670 7634; www.odessa.ie; 13-14 Dame Ct; 🕑 6-11pm Tue-Sun, plus 11.30am-4.30pm Sat & Sun; 🚍 all city-centre; 🚼

Join the city's hipsters for homemade burgers, steaks or daily fish specials in Odessa's loungey atmosphere, complete with comfy sofas and retro lamps. Now with private member's club upstairs, you can celeb-watch through the window and weep. Weekend brunch is extremely popular: you were warned.

🍴 SEAGRASS

Mediterranean €€

☎ 478 9595; www.seagrassdublin.com; 30 S Richmond St; 🕑 6-11pm; 🚍 16, 19, 122; 🆅

Utterly unassuming from the outside, this excellent new spot in the south of the district will surprise you: the locally sourced, roughly Mediterranean menu (baked seafood penne, pan-fried lambs' livers, and a bacon and cabbage risotto are typical) is uniformly excellent, the dining room is quietly elegant and the service absolutely perfect.

🍴 SHEBEEN CHIC

Modern Irish €€

☎ 679 9667; 5 S Great George's St; 🕑 noon-10pm Sun-Wed, to 11pm Thu-Sat; 🚍 16, 19, 83

The menu reads like it was written by Tom Waits: 'spudballs with broccoli, mushrooms and auld cheddar,' or 'leek, spud and maybe mud' are representatives of a cuisine best described as Irish with attitude. In the basement is a bar with a speakeasy vibe.

🍴 SILK ROAD CAFE

Middle Eastern €€

☎ 407 0770; www.silkroadcafe.ie; Chester Beatty Library, Dublin Castle; 🕑 11am-4pm Mon-Fri; 🚍 50, 51b, 77, 78a, 123; 🆅

Museum cafes don't often make you salivate, but this little Middle

Eastern–North African–Mediterranean gem is the exception. The menu is about two-thirds veggie, with Greek moussaka and spinach lasagne house specialities complementing the deep-fried chickpeas and hummus starters. For dessert, there's Lebanese baklava and coconut *kataïfi* (angel-hair pastry). All dishes are halal and kosher.

🍽 SIMON'S PLACE *Cafe*   €
☎ 679 7821; George's St Arcade;
🕑 8.30am-6pm Mon-Sat;
🚌 all city-centre; **V**

Simon hasn't had to change the menu of doorstep sandwiches and wholesome vegetarian soups since he first opened shop two decades ago, and why should he? His grub is as heartening and legendary as he is. It's a great place to mull over a coffee and watch life go by in the old-fashioned arcade.

🍽 UKIYO
Japanese & Korean   €€
☎ 633 4071; www.ukiyobar.com; 7-9 Exchequer St; karaoke room per hr €25;
🕑 noon-4pm, 5pm-midnight Mon-Thu, to 3am Fri-Sun; 🚌 all city-centre; **V**

Tasty grub like *kim chi ji gae* (a stew made with cabbage) and *saba tatsuta age* (deep-fried mackerel) are reason enough to put this trendy restaurant on your radar, but Dubliners love this place for its karaoke rooms downstairs and its

weekend 'club' nights – basically a gathering of music lovers having a few drinks and enjoying the excellent tunes laid down by the DJs.

🍸 DRINK
🍸 ANSEO *Bar*
18 Lower Camden St; 🚌 16, 83, 123

This place might not look much on the outside, or the inside for that matter – with its bog-standard carpet and chrome decor – but those underground scenesters Monkey Tennis work their magic on Friday nights, rocking the house with everything from Hot Chip to Velvet Underground.

🍸 BAR WITH NO NAME *Bar*
☎ 675 3708; 3 Fade St; 🚌 all city-centre

A low-key entrance just next to L'Gueuleton leads upstairs to one of the nicest bar spaces in town – three huge rooms in a restored Victorian townhouse plus a sizeable heated patio area for smokers. There's no sign or name – folks just refer to it as the bar with no name or, if you're a real insider, Number 3.

🍸 BERNARD SHAW *Pub*
☎ 085 712 8342; 11-12 S Richmond St;
🚌 16, 19, 122

It mightn't look like much and it might smell a bit, but there's no mistaking the ubercool status of this old-style pub since it was taken over by the Bodytonic production crew, who've installed nightly DJs playing anything from dub reggae to ambient electronica.

☝ BIA BAR Bar
☎ 405 3563; 30 Lower Stephen St; 🚌 83, 123, 🚇 St Stephen's Green
These folks know how to keep a punter coming back: fast and friendly staff, DJs, a young eye-candy crowd and, most important-ly, one of the centre's biggest beer gardens, complete with pebbled floor and palm trees.

☝ DRAGON Bar
☎ 478 1590; 64-65 S Great George's St; 🕐 5-11.30pm Mon-Wed, to 2.30am Thu-Sat, to 11pm Sun; 🚌 all city-centre

The latest addition to Dublin's gay scene, this disco bar with colourful Asian decor, comfy booths and small dance floor attracts young pre-George (below) revellers.

☝ GEORGE Bar
☎ 478 2983; 89 S Great George's St; admission most nights after 10pm €5-8; 🕐 12.30-11.30pm Mon & Tue, to 3am Wed-Sat, to 1am Sun; 🚌 all city-centre
You can't miss the bright-purple George, Dublin's best-known gay bar, which has a reputation for becoming ever-more wild and wacky as the night progresses. At 6.30pm on Sunday it is packed for an enormously popular bingo night, while Thursday night is the

Calling the bingo balls – legs eleven? – on Sunday night at the George

Missing Link game show hosted by Annie Balls.

Y GLOBE *Bar*
☎ 671 1220; 11 S Great George's St; 🚌 all city-centre

Dublin's original and best cafe-bar is a mecca for hip young locals and clued-in visitors. With its wooden floors and brick walls, it's as much a daytime haunt for a good latte as a watering hole by night. Eclectic music, Sunday-afternoon jazz and friendly staff help the place thrive. It has recently changed hands, but the new owners will hardly try to fix what ain't broke.

Y GROGAN'S CASTLE LOUNGE *Bar*
☎ 677 9320; 15 S William St; 🚌 all city-centre, 🚇 St Stephen's Green

Known simply as Grogan's (after the original owner), this old place is a city-centre institution. Long patronised by writers, painters and other bohemian types (whose work it often displays on the walls), it's laid-back and contemplative much of the day. Oddly, drinks are slightly cheaper in the stone-floor bar than in the carpeted lounge.

Y LONG HALL *Pub*
☎ 475 1590; 51 S Great George's St; 🚌 16, 16a, 19, 19a, 65, 83

With wildly ornate Victorian woodwork, mirrors and chandeliers, this is one of the city's most beautiful and best-loved pubs. From musk-coloured walls to mirrored columns behind the bar, it's all elegantly dingy. The bartenders are experts at their craft, an increasingly rare sight in Dublin these days.

Y MARKET BAR *Bar*
☎ 613 9094; 14a Fade St; 🚌 all city-centre

High ceilings, bench seating, potted plants and the din of a chatty crowd give this huge former sausage factory the atmosphere of Grand Central Station on Christmas Eve. It's fashionable and friendly, the tapas from the open kitchen are great, and staff even bring drinks to your table. Check out the wonderful bar made from dipped-brass bank doors.

Y SOLAS *Bar*
☎ 478 0583; 31 Wexford St; 🕐 9.30am-12.30am Sun-Wed, to 1.30am Thu-Sat; 🚌 83, 121

Wexford and Camden Sts have become the golden mile of the Dublin indie scene, with dark and loungey Solas playing a prominent role. Late opening, nightly DJs, a funky rooftop beer garden and its proximity to Whelans and the Village all add to its vibe. Oh, and of course the loos that flush rain water.

▼ STAG'S HEAD *Trad Music Pub*
☎ 679 3701; 1 Dame Ct;
🚌 all city-centre

Built in 1770 but remodelled in 1895 at the height of Victorian opulence, this pub has magnificent stained glass, chandeliers and marble, carved wood and, of course, mounted stags' heads. It can get crowded but it's worth it; the food's pretty good, too.

⭐ PLAY

⭐ ANDREW'S LANE THEATRE
Club

☎ 478 0766; www.andrewslane.com;
St Andrew's La; admission €5-10;
🕑 10.30pm-3am Thu-Sun;
🚌 all city-centre

Club purists will enjoy ALT's stripped-down look, which includes a huge dance floor, a kick-ass sound system and a regular menu of visiting DJs and live gigs.

⭐ CRAWDADDY *Live Music*
☎ 478 0166; www.pod.ie; Harcourt St;
🕑 7.30pm-3am Wed-Sat;
🚌 14, 15, 48a; 🚊 Harcourt

Named after the London club where the Stones launched their professional careers in 1963, Crawdaddy is an intimate bar-venue that specialises in putting on rootsy performers – from African drum bands to avant-garde jazz artists and flamenco guitarists.

⭐ JJ SMYTH'S *Live Music*
☎ 475 2565; www.jjsmyths.com;
12 Aungier St; admission €8-10;
🕑 most shows start 8.30-9.30pm;
🚌 16, 16a, 19, 19a, 65, 83

Jazz and blues at this small but legendary pub draw a regular crowd. The Irish Blues Club plays on Tuesday and long-standing resident bands as well as international guest acts play every other night except Wednesday.

⭐ RÍ RÁ *Club*
☎ 677 4835; www.rira.ie; Dame Ct;
admission free, special events €5-11;
🕑 11.30pm-3am Mon-Sat;
🚌 all city-centre

This long-established club changed hands in 2007, but the new owners are bent on continuing the long-standing commitment to music without frenetic beats – for now, at least. The emphasis has long been on funky stuff, from soul to hip-hop, but there's plenty of rock thrown in.

⭐ TRIPOD *Club & Live Music*
☎ 478 0166; www.pod.ie; 35 Harcourt St; admission €5-20; 🕑 11pm-3am Thu-Sat; 🚌 14, 15, 65, 83, 🚊 Harcourt

Launched in late 2006 in the atmospheric old Harcourt St station, Tripod integrates three venues (geddit?): a state-of-the-art 1300-capacity live rock and pop music venue, a smaller dance

A Tripod DJ keeps the tracks coming

club and the intimate live venue Crawdaddy (opposite).

⭐ VILLAGE *Live Music*
☎ 475 8555; www.thevillagevenue.com; 26 Wexford St; 🕐 noon-2.30am Mon-Sat, noon-1am Sun; 🚌 16, 16a, 19, 19a, 65, 83
This large venue is surprisingly cosy for its size. All wooden cladding and warm lighting, the free downstairs bar packs 'em in for its late licence. Upstairs, the venue puts on medium-sized international and home-grown rock and pop acts most nights.

⭐ WHELANS *Live Music*
☎ 478 0766; www.whelanslive.com; 25 Wexford St; admission €10-25; 🕐 doors open 8pm; 🚌 14, 15, 65, 83
A good gig here can be quite magical. The crowd gathers round the elevated central stage and more peer down from the circular balcony – everyone mouthing the words to their favourite songs and ballads. Whelans offers an interesting parade of fine local and international acts and singer-songwriters – well worth a look. Enter via Camden Row.

KILMAINHAM & THE LIBERTIES

>KILMAINHAM & THE LIBERTIES

Light on entertainment but laden with sights, Kilmainham and the Liberties are among the oldest districts in Dublin. Here you'll find the city's two cathedrals - one, Christ Church, was built firmly within what was then the medieval city walls, while the other, St Patrick's, was outside of them. The latter was part of the Liberties, Dublin's oldest surviving and most staunchly traditional neighbourhood. Walking here you may detect a curious aroma in the air: the smell of roasting hops, used in the production of Guinness. For many visitors, Dublin's black gold is the epitome of all things Irish, making the Guinness Storehouse the city's most visited tourist attraction. Further along from the famous brewery is Kilmainham, home to the hulking prison that was central to the struggle for Irish independence (and a city highlight) and an ancient soldiers' hospital, now the country's most important modern art museum.

KILMAINHAM & THE LIBERTIES

👁 SEE
Bad Art Gallery **1** E3
Christ Church Cathedral .. **2** F2
Cross Gallery **3** E2
Dublinia & the Viking
   World **4** F2
Guinness Storehouse **5** D2
Irish Museum of
   Modern Art **6** B2
James Joyce House of
   the Dead **7** E1

Kilmainham Gaol **8** A2
Marsh's Library **9** F3
St Audoen's Protestant
   Church **10** E2
St Patrick's
   Cathedral **11** F3

🏠 SHOP
Design Associates **12** E2
Fleury Antiques **13** F3

O'Sullivan Antiques **14** E2
Oxfam Home **15** E3

🍸 DRINK
Brazen Head **16** E2

⭐ PLAY
Vicar St **17** E2

SEE

BAD ART GALLERY

☎ 087 991 0650; www.thebadartgallery
dublin.com; 79 Francis St; admission free;
⏰ 10.30am-6pm Mon-Sat, 2-5pm Sun;
🚌 51b, 78a, 121, 123

This tongue-in-cheek gallery for emerging students and contemporary Irish artists specialises in big, bold and affordable art. Deborah Donnelly paints brash, colourful portraits of cows, cakes and circus tents. Get there for opening nights when the room is flamboyantly dressed.

CHRIST CHURCH CATHEDRAL

☎ 677 8099; www.cccdub.ie; Christ Church Pl; admission €6/3; ⏰ 9.45am-4.15pm Mon-Sat, 12.30-2.30pm Sun Sep-May, 9.45am-6.15pm Mon, Tue & Fri, to 4.15pm Wed, Thu & Sat, 12.30-2.30pm & 4.30-6.15pm Sun Jun–mid-Jul, 9.45am-6.15pm Mon-Fri, to 4.15pm Sat, 12.30-2.30pm & 4.30-6.15pm Sun mid-Jul–Aug; 🚌 50, 66, 77, 121, 123

Dublin's most imposing church and famed landmark, Christ Church Cathedral lies within the city's original Norse settlement and the old heart of medieval Dublin. It was commissioned in 1172 by the Anglo-Norman conqueror of Dublin, Richard de Clare – 'Strongbow' – whose tomb is just inside the main door, and

> ### THE BELLS, THE BELLS
> The melodic sound of Christ Church's bells has been ringing through the Dublin air since 1670. Nineteen bells, the greatest number rung in this way worldwide and weighing up to 2.25 tonnes each, are hand rung in a mathematical sequence, with training taking years to complete.

Archbishop Laurence O'Toole. Try to visit just before choral evensong to catch the choir's wonderfully evocative recitals, which bring the cathedral's rich atmosphere to life.

CROSS GALLERY

☎ 473 8978; www.crossgallery.ie; 59 Francis St; admission free; ⏰ 10am-5.30pm Tue-Fri, 11am-3pm Sat; 🚌 51b, 78a, 121, 123

Nestled amid the top-end antique stores of the Liberties, Cross is an open-plan gallery in a terraced house designed to be unintimidating (in both design and price) to first-time buyers. Contemporary and abstract artists such as Clea Van der Grijn, Simon English and Laurent Mellet are represented.

DUBLINIA & THE VIKING WORLD

☎ 679 4611; www.dublinia.ie; admission €6/3.75/17; ⏰ 10am-5pm Apr-Sep, 11am-4pm Mon-Sat & 10am-4.30pm Sun Oct-Mar; 🚌 51b, 78a, 123; ♿

A must for the kids, the old Synod Hall attached to Christ Church Cathedral is home to this seemingly perennial exhibit on medieval Dublin, complete with models, music, streetscapes and interactive displays. The newly added Viking World tells the story of Dublin's 9th- and 10th-century Scandinavian invaders and the city they built in their wake. Finally, you can climb neighbouring St Michael's Tower for views over the city to the Dublin Hills.

◉ GUINNESS STOREHOUSE
☎ 408 4800; www.guinness-storehouse.com; St James's Gate; admission €15/11, under 6yr free; ⏱ 9.30am-5pm Sep-Jun, 9.30am-7pm Jul-Aug; 🚌 51b, 78a, 123; 🚊 St James's

Like Disneyland for beer lovers, the Guinness Storehouse is an all-singing, all-dancing extravaganza combining sophisticated exhibits with more than a pintful of marketing. The highlight of a visit to the museum – housed in an old grain store opposite the original St James's Gate Brewery – is a glass of Guinness in the Gravity Bar at the top of the building. Check online for admission discounts. See also p12.

◉ IRISH MUSEUM OF MODERN ART (IMMA)
☎ 612 9900; www.imma.ie; Military Rd; admission free; ⏱ 10am-5.30pm Tue-Sat, noon-5.30pm Sun; 🚌 26, 51, 78a, 79, 90, 123

Ireland's premier gallery of contemporary art is at the Royal

Once the Royal Hospital Kilmainham, this graceful building now houses the Irish Museum of Modern Art

Hospital, Kilmainham, a striking 17th-century building whose design is inspired by Les Invalides in Paris and which served the same purpose, as a hospice for retired soldiers. Even if contemporary art doesn't float your boat, a wander around this extraordinary building is a must. See also p17.

JAMES JOYCE HOUSE OF THE DEAD

☎ 672 8008; 15 Usher's Quay; admission €10/8, under 6yr free; ⏱ 10am-5pm; 🚌 25x, 26, 46a, 78, 79, 90, 92

The restoration of the setting for James Joyce's story *The Dead* has been a labour of love for barrister Brendan Kilty. As a museum there aren't many actual artefacts (besides touring exhibitions) but walking through the crumbling

rooms that are almost as they were when Joyce spent Christmases there with his aunts is very special.

KILMAINHAM GAOL

☎ 453 5984; www.heritageireland .com; Inchicore Rd; admission €6/2; ⏱ 9.30am-5pm Apr-Oct, 9.30am-4pm Mon-Sat, 10am-4pm Sun Nov-Mar; 🚌 26, 51, 78a, 79, 90, 123

One of Dublin's most sobering sights, Kilmainham Gaol oozes centuries of pain, oppression and suffering from its decrepit limestone hulk. Scene of countless emotional episodes along Ireland's rocky road to independence, the jail was home to many of the country's political heroes, martyrs and villains. Enjoy the visit! For more, see p18.

MARSH'S LIBRARY

☎ 454 3511; www.marshlibrary.ie; St Patrick's Close; admission €2.50/1.50; ⏱ 10am-1pm & 2-5pm Mon & Wed-Fri, 10.30am-1pm Sat; 🚌 50, 50a, 54, 54a, 56a

Virtually unchanged for 300 years, Marsh's Library is a glorious example of an 18th-century scholar's den. In fact, it is one of the few buildings from that time that still retains its original usage. The beautiful, dark oak bookcases, each topped with elaborately carved and gilded gables, are filled with some 25,000 books dating from the 15th to the early 18th century.

A SCHOLASTIC SOLOMON

Englishman Narcissus Marsh (1638–1713), an Oxford graduate and Archbishop of Armagh and Dublin and six times Lord Justice of Ireland, must have been a formidable chap. As provost of Trinity College he was an ardent supporter of the Irish language and, believing that knowledge is king, was shocked to find there was nowhere in Ireland for the public to read. His library became a repository for his fine collection of books to advance the minds of his host nation.

Sineád Gleeson
Music journalist, blogger and arts columnist for, among others, the Irish Times

Favourite neighbourhood I love poking about in the dusty corners of a city, and there's none more fascinating than the nooks and crannies within the triangle between St Patrick's Cathedral (p102), Dublin Castle (p79) and Christ Church Cathedral (p98). I lived for years opposite St Patrick's, and I did so much exploring that the area has seeped permanently into my consciousness!

Favourite spot If I had to pick one, it would be the steps of Hoey's Court (Map pp80–1, B2), which is not just where Jonathan Swift was born, but is one of the most filmic spots in the whole city – it wouldn't look out of place in a Hitchcock classic. When I was younger the alley was closed to the public by a set of wrought-iron gates – which made it even more of a corner of mystery.

◉ ST AUDOEN'S PROTESTANT CHURCH

☎ 677 0088; Cornmarket, High St;
🕑 9.30am-4.45pm Jun-Sep;
🚌 51b, 78a, 123, 206

The only surviving medieval parish church in the city, St Audoen's was built between 1181 and 1212, though the site is thought to be much older. Enlarged in its 15th-century heyday, it shrank to its present size in the 18th and 19th centuries, when the eastern wing and St Anne's Chapel were left to ruin. Today the chapel houses an excellent visitor centre, and sometimes runs guided tours.

◉ ST PATRICK'S CATHEDRAL

☎ 475 4817; www.stpatrickscathedral
.ie; St Patrick's Close; admission €5.50/4.50;
🕑 9am-6pm Mon-Sat, 9-11am, 12.45-3pm
& 4.15-6pm Sun Mar-Oct, 9am-6pm Mon-
Fri, 9am-5pm Sat, 10-11am & 12.45-3pm
Sun Nov-Feb; 🚌 49, 50, 54a, 56a, 77

This cathedral, which is located a mere stone's throw from its sibling Christ Church, smack-bang in the heart of old Dublin, stands where St Patrick himself is said to have baptised converts at a well – even if the story isn't exactly verifiable and the church itself in fact dates from 1191. What is proven fact, however, is that during his 1649 'visit' to

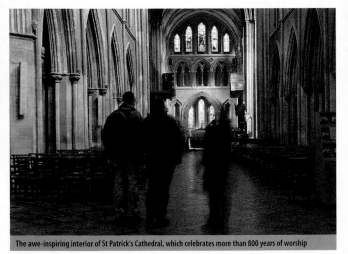

The awe-inspiring interior of St Patrick's Cathedral, which celebrates more than 800 years of worship

Ireland, the one and only Oliver Cromwell converted the nave into a stable for his horses.

SHOP

DESIGN ASSOCIATES
Antiques & Home Decor
☎ 453 7767; 144-145 Francis St;
🕑 9.30am-6pm Mon-Sat;
🚌 123, 206, 51b
Choose from high-end antiques, marble statues, beautiful contemporary lamps and glass work in this tasteful interior-design shop.

FLEURY ANTIQUES *Antiques*
☎ 473 0878; 57 Francis St; 🕑 9.30am-6pm Mon-Sat; 🚌 123, 206, 51b
Fleury specialises in oil paintings, vases, candelabras, porcelain, silverware and decorative pieces from the 18th century to the 1930s.

O'SULLIVAN ANTIQUES
Antiques
☎ 454 1143; 43-44 Francis St; 🕑 10am-5pm Mon-Sat; 🚌 123, 206, 51b
Specialising in fine Georgian, Victorian and Edwardian period furniture, you're also likely to come across distinctive ceramics, crystal, medals and costumes.

OXFAM HOME *Charity Shop*
☎ 402 0555; 86 Francis St; 🕑 10am-5.30pm Mon-Fri, 10am-1pm Sat;
🚌 123, 206, 51b

They say charity begins at home, so get rummaging among the veneer off casts in this furniture branch of the charity chain where you might stumble across the odd 1960s Subbuteo table or art deco dresser. Esoteric vinyl from the '80s is another speciality of the house.

DRINK

BRAZEN HEAD
Trad Music Pub
☎ 679 5186; 20 Lower Bridge St; 🚌 134
Reputed to be Dublin's oldest pub, the Brazen Head was founded in 1198, but the present building is a young thing, dating from only 1668. Attracting foreign students and tourists as well as locals, the pub has traditional Irish music nightly, usually kicking off at 9pm.

PLAY

VICAR STREET
Comedy & Live Music
☎ 454 5533; www.vicarstreet.com;
58-59 Thomas St; 🚌 51b, 78a, 123, 206
Smaller rock, folk and comedy performances take place at this venue near Christ Church Cathedral. Though it seats 1000 between its table-serviced area and theatre-style balcony, it retains an intimate atmosphere, with low lighting and an excellent sound system. Neil Young, Bob Dylan and Justin Timberlake have all played here.

>O'CONNELL STREET & AROUND

The imperially wide O'Connell St is the centre of Dublin and its most historically important thoroughfare. It became Dublin's main street in 1794, when O'Connell Bridge was built and the city's axis shifted east. The north side was the residential area of choice at the start of the Georgian period, but when the hoi polloi got too close, the aristocracy doubled back over the Liffey and settled the new areas surrounding Leinster House.

Although it has lost much of its commercial and symbolic pre-eminence to Grafton St and the southside, a massive program of urban rejuvenation has seen the grand old dame recapture some of her former polish, thanks in no small measure to the growing multi-ethnicity of Dublin, which has seen recent arrivals bring new vitality to the surrounding streets.

O'CONNELL STREET & AROUND

🔵 SEE
Custom House	**1**	F3
Dublin City Gallery – Hugh Lane	**2**	C1
Dublin Writers Museum	**3**	C1
Garden of Remembrance	**4**	C1
General Post Office	**5**	D3
James Joyce Cultural Centre	**6**	D1
Jeanie Johnston	**7**	F3
St Mary's Pro-Cathedral	**8**	D2

🏠 SHOP
Arnott's	**9**	C3
Debenham's	**10**	C3
Dublin City Gallery – Hugh Lane Shop	(see 2)	
Dublin Woollen Mills	**11**	C4
Early Learning Centre	**12**	C3
Irish Historical Picture Company	**13**	D4
Jervis Centre	**14**	C3
Louis Copeland	**15**	B3
Moore Street Market	**16**	C2
Penney's	**17**	D3
Smyths Toys	**18**	C3
Winding Stair	(see 26)	

🍴 EAT
101 Talbot	**19**	E2
Bar Italia	**20**	C4
Bon Ga	**21**	B3
Chapter One	(see 3)	
Cobalt Café & Gallery	**22**	D1
La Taverna di Bacco	**23**	C4
Melody	**24**	B3
Soup Dragon	**25**	B4
Winding Stair	**26**	C4

🍸 DRINK
Church	**27**	C3
Flowing Tide	**28**	D3
Sackville Lounge	**29**	D3
Sin É	**30**	B4

⭐ PLAY
Abbey Theatre	**31**	E3
Ambassador Theatre	**32**	D2
Cineworld	**33**	B3
Gate Theatre	**34**	D2
Laughter Lounge	**35**	D3
Panti Bar	**36**	B4
Twisted Pepper	**37**	D3

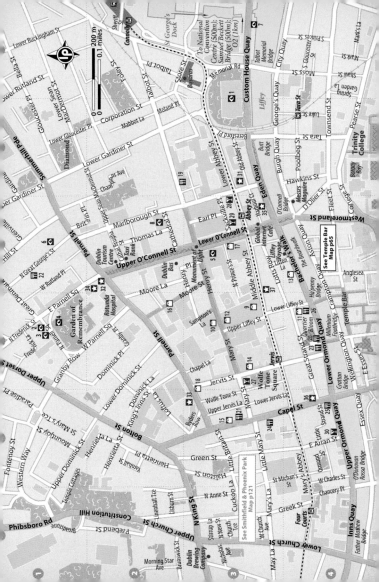

NEIGHBOURHOODS

O'CONNELL STREET & AROUND

👁 SEE

☉ CUSTOM HOUSE

☎ 888 2538; Custom House Quay; admission €1; 🕓 10am-12.30pm Mon-Fri, 2-5pm Sat & Sun mid-Mar–Oct, closed Mon, Tue & Sat Nov–mid-Mar; 🚆 Connolly, 🚆 Tara St

A Dublin landmark, the Custom House was built to accommodate the city's tax commissioners. James Gandon's first architectural triumph, the 18th-century building has a copper dome set above clock faces and neoclassical columns typical of the era. While the building now houses the Department of the Environment, the visitor centre explains its history.

HUGH LANE HITS

> *Waterloo Bridge,* Monet
> *Parapluies,* Renoir
> *Blue and White,* William Scott
> *Sandra,* Sean Scully

☉ DUBLIN CITY GALLERY – HUGH LANE

☎ 874 1903; www.hughlane.ie; 22 N Parnell Sq; admission free; 🕓 10am-6pm Tue-Thu, 10am-5pm Fri & Sat, 11am-5pm Sun, guided tours 11am Tue & 1.30pm Sun; 🚌 3, 10, 16, 19, 123, 🚆 Connolly; ♿

Whatever reputation Dublin has as a repository of world-class art has a lot to do with the simply stun-

Dublin's City Gallery houses almost 2000 permanent artworks alongside dynamic temporary exhibitions

MONUMENTAL FAILURES

Dublin's history is littered with public monuments that have been blown up, defaced, ridiculed and bungled. William III's statue on College Green was mutilated so often it was sold for scrap in 1929, as was one of George II soon after. In 1957, Lord Gough was blown off his horse in Phoenix Park, and in 1966 Lord Nelson's head exploded onto the footpath on O'Connell St. At the north end of Grafton St, the statue of Molly Malone (Map p39, C2) with unlikely plunging neckline, represents the legendary cockles and mussels vendor who is the subject of Dublin's most famous song.

Dublin's last big civic project, the 120m-high spire sculpture, the Monument of Light (Map p105, D3) replaced Nelson's Column on O'Connell St. Heated debate about its 'purpose' delayed its scheduled erection for millennium New Year's Eve by three years, though now most Dubliners appreciate its beauty, the scorn long forgotten.

ning collection at this exquisite gallery. Its collection bridges the gap between the National Gallery's old masters and the cutting-edge works on show at the Irish Museum of Modern Art. One highlight is the Francis Bacon studio, painstakingly moved in all its shambolic mess from the artist's London home.

◉ DUBLIN WRITERS MUSEUM

☎ 872 2077; www.writersmuseum.com; 18 N Parnell Sq; admission €7.50/6.30; ⊗ 10am-5pm Mon-Sat Sep-May, to 6pm Jun-Aug, 11am-5pm Sun year-round; ☐ 11, 13, 16, 19, 36, 40, ☒ Connolly
You'd think that Dublin's rich and extensive literary tradition would ensure that a museum devoted to some of Ireland's greatest scribblers would be a real treat. But somehow this museum full

of vaguely literary ephemera is something of a damp squib, unless Samuel Beckett's phone from his Paris apartment or Brendan Behan's union card will tickle your fancy.

◉ GARDEN OF REMEMBRANCE

☎ 874 3074; www.heritageireland.ie; Parnell Sq; admission free; ⊗ 9.30am-dusk May-Sep, from 11am Oct-Apr; ☐ 36, 40, ☒ Connolly
Established for the 50th anniversary of the 1916 Easter Rising, this peaceful garden commemorates those who sacrificed their lives in the long struggle for Irish independence. The centrepiece is a 1971 sculpture by Oisin Kelly depicting the myth of the Children of Lir, who were turned into swans by their wicked stepmother.

NEIGHBOURHOODS

O'CONNELL STREET & AROUND

The calm interior of the General Post Office belies its spirited past

⊙ GENERAL POST OFFICE

☎ 705 7000; www.anpost.ie; Lower O'Connell St; admission free; ⏱ 8am-8pm Mon-Sat; 🚌 O'Connell St, 🚆 Abbey St

Talk about going postal. The GPO will forever be linked to the dramatic events of Irish independence. The 1916 Easter Rising leaders read their proclamation of a republic from its steps, and the facade is still pockmarked from the subsequent clash from fighting during the Civil War in 1922. Today the GPO still attracts protesting pressure groups and individuals on a personal crusade.

⊙ JAMES JOYCE CULTURAL CENTRE

☎ 878 8547; www.jamesjoyce.ie; 35 N Great George's St; admission €5/4; ⏱ 10am-5pm Tue-Sat; 🚌 3, 10, 11, 13, 16, 19, 22, 123, 🚆 Connolly

For anyone whose unthumbed copy of *Ulysses* is still gathering dust on the bedside table, get to grips with the text using new user-friendly interactive displays that demystify the work. The revamped centre in a fabulous Georgian house (location of *Ulysses* dance instructor Denis Maginni's classes) explores the great scribe's life through letters and memorabilia. The centre, not to be confused with the James Joyce Museum (p129), also runs Joyce tours.

JEANIE JOHNSTON
☎ 066-712 9999; www.jeaniejohnston .ie; Custom House Quay; admission €5/3; 10.30am-5pm Sat & Sun Oct-Apr; Connolly, Tara St

One of the city's most original tourist attractions is an exact, working replica of a 19th-century 'coffin ship,' as the sailing boats that transported starving emigrants away from Ireland during the Famine were gruesomely known. The ship also operates as a sail training vessel, with journeys taking place from May to September. If you are visiting during these times, check the website for details of when it will be in dock.

LOCATION! LOCATION!
Some say the city of Dublin, its streets, squares and buildings – not Leopold Bloom – is the most important character in *Ulysses*. Joyce claimed that if the city ever disappeared, he hoped it could be reconstructed from the detail in his book. The story follows a single day, 16 June 1904, in Bloom's life as he walks and rides in trams and carriages around 30km of Dublin streets from Dalkey to 7 Eccles St, now site of the Mater Private Hospital.

ST MARY'S PRO-CATHEDRAL
☎ 874 5441; www.procathedral.ie; 83 Marlborough St; 8am-7pm Mon-Sat, 8am-2pm Sun; 27, 31b, 42a, 42b, 130, Abbey St

Dublin's Catholic cathedral is tucked away on Marlborough St – a deliberately inconspicuous site. Built between 1816 and 1825, the cathedral's facade is modelled on the Temple of Hephaestus in Athens and its carved altar is also very impressive. Oddly, Marlborough St was once the biggest red-light district in Europe…

SHOP
ARNOTT'S *Department Store*
☎ 805 0400; Middle Abbey St; 9am-6.30pm Mon-Wed, Fri & Sat, to 9pm Thu, noon-6pm Sun; O'Connell St, Jervis

Occupying a huge block with entry on Henry, Liffey and Abbey Sts, this grand dame is one of Dublin's best department stores. From contemporary garden furniture to high fashion, it's all here, and there's a great selection of kids' designer gear on the 1st floor.

DEBENHAM'S
Department Store
☎ 873 0044; 83 Henry St; 9am-6.30pm Mon-Wed, Fri & Sat, to 9pm Thu, noon-6pm Sun; O'Connell St, Jervis

In 2006, the English chain bought out one of Dublin's oldest and grandest department stores and went on where Roches Stores had left off: bold and glass-fronted on the outside and street-smart fashion labels such as Zara, Warehouse and G-Star on the inside, as well as the obligatory home wares and electrical sections.

🅲 DUBLIN CITY GALLERY – HUGH LANE SHOP
Museum Shop

☎ 874 1903; Charlemont House, N Parnell Sq; 🕒 9.30am-6pm Tue-Thu, to 5pm Fri & Sat, 11am-5pm Sun; 🚌 3, 10, 16, 19, 123, 🚆 Connolly

You could waste some wonderful time in this almost-secret cultural playground, digging out cubist fridge magnets, huge po-mo hanging mobiles, colour-by-number masterpieces, cloth puppets, unusual wooden toys and beautiful art and pop-culture hardbacks.

🅲 DUBLIN WOOLLEN MILLS
Clothing & Accessories

☎ 677 5014; 41 Lower Ormond Quay; 🕒 9.30am-6pm Mon-Wed, Fri & Sat, to 7.30pm Thu, 1-6pm Sun; 🚌 all cross-city, 🚆 Jervis

Situated at the northern end of Ha'penny Bridge, this is one of Dublin's major wool outlets. It features a large selection of traditional sweaters, cardigans, scarves, rugs, shawls and other woollen goods, and runs a tax-free shopping scheme.

🅲 EARLY LEARNING CENTRE
Toys

☎ 873 1945; 3 Henry St; 🕒 9am-5pm Mon-Wed & Fri, to 8pm Thu, to 5.30pm Sat, 1-5pm Sun; 🚌 all cross-city, 🚆 Jervis

Fun with an educational bent for the tiniest tots, including ELC-brand plastic and wooden toys, spelling and numerical games, simple devices that honk and squeak and a good range of Thomas the Tank Engine stuff.

🅲 IRISH HISTORICAL PICTURE COMPANY *Photography*

☎ 872 0144; 5 Lower Ormond Quay; 🕒 9am-6pm Mon-Fri, 10am-5pm Sat & Sun; 🚌 all cross-city, 🚆 Jervis

With a print collection that's second only to the holdings at the National Library, this place has more than 12,000 pictures taken around Ireland at the turn of the 20th century. The prints cover all 32 counties and range from town streetscapes to images of bog cutters. Mounted prints can be framed within minutes.

🅲 JERVIS CENTRE
Shopping Centre

☎ 878 1323; Jervis St; 🕒 9am-6pm Mon-Wed, Fri & Sat, to 9pm Thu, noon-6pm Sun; 🚆 Jervis

An ultramodern, domed mall that's a veritable shrine to the British chain store. Boots, Top Shop, Debenhams, Argos, Dixons, M&S and Miss Selfridge all get a look in.

🎬 LOUIS COPELAND
Men's Clothing
☎ 872 1600; 39-41 Capel St; ⏰ 9am-5.30pm Mon-Wed, Fri & Sat, to 7.30pm Thu; 🚌 37, 70, 134, 172, 🚇 Jervis
A Dublin tradition for off-the-peg suits and casual menswear, with Lacoste, Burberry, Dior and Louis Féraud. Copeland himself works at the original Capel St store; there are two others including

one at 18-19 Wicklow St (Map p39, C2).

🎬 MOORE STREET MARKET
Market
Moore St; ⏰ 9am-4pm Mon-Sat; 🚌 all cross-city, 🚇 Jervis
An open-air, steadfastly 'Old Dublin' market, with fruit, fish and flowers on offer. Traditional vendors hawk cheap cigarettes, tobacco and chocolate among the new wave of Nigerians and Chinese selling phone cards and hair extensions. Don't try to buy just one banana though – if the sign says 10 for €1, that's what it is.

Tomatoes in abundance at the Moore Street Market

WORTH THE TRIP: CLONTARF, HOWTH & MALAHIDE

From north of the Liffey you can travel east, hugging the harbour, to a number of attractive water-side stops. First up is Clontarf, a pretty bayside suburb whose main enticements are birds and golf. The **North Bull Wall**, which extends about 1km into Dublin Bay, was built in 1820 to stop Dublin Harbour from silting up. Marshes and dunes developed behind the wall, creating **North Bull Island**, which is now a Unesco biosphere reserve. The bird population can reach 40,000 – watch for shelducks, curlews and oystercatchers on the mud flats – and a range of plants and other animals can be seen. An **interpretive centre** (☎ 833 8341; admission free; ✆ times vary, call ahead) on the island is reached by walking across the 1.5km-long northern causeway.

Two lovely seaside villages sit on Dublin Bay's northern end. Howth (rhymes with 'both') has a pleasant port with three piers, some good pubs and excellent fish and chip joints. Looming above it is the **Hill of Howth**, wonderful for a leisurely half- or full-day's walk with views of Dublin city and the bay.

About 1.5km offshore is **Ireland's Eye**, a rocky seabird sanctuary with the ruins of a 6th-century monastery. There's a Martello tower at the island's northwestern end, while at the eastern end a spectacular rock face plummets into the sea. Seals can also be spotted. **Doyle & Sons** (☎ 831 4200) runs boats out to the island from the East Pier of Howth Harbour during summer from around 10.30am on weekends. Return trips cost €10.

Malahide's main attraction is **Malahide Castle** (☎ 846 2184; admission €6.70/5.70), set in 1 sq km of parklands. The castle served as the Talbot family home from 1185 to 1976 and incorporates a hotchpotch of architectural styles. On the grounds is the **Fry Model Railway** and **Tara's Palace** (☎ 846 3779; admission by donation; ✆ 10.45am-4.45pm Mon-Sat, 11.30am-5.30pm Sun Apr-Sep), an elaborate, oversized doll's house. The **Talbot Botanic Gardens** (☎ 872 7777; admission €4; ✆ 2-5pm May-Sep), also within the estate's grounds, has a varied collection of plants, many from the southern hemisphere.

Coming to land at Ireland's Eye beneath its historic Martello tower

🖿 PENNEY'S *Clothing*
☎ 872 0466; 37 O'Connell St;
🕑 8.30am-6.30pm Mon-Wed, Fri & Sat,
to 9pm Thu, noon-6pm Sun; 🚇 O'Connell
St, 🚊 Abbey St
The clothes might not withstand
industrial washing, but who cares
when they only cost €3? Penney's
attraction is its bright up-to-the-
minute tops, funky underwear and
knits for adults and juniors.

🖿 SMYTHS TOYS *Toys*
☎ 878 2878; Jervis St; 🕑 10am-6pm
Mon-Wed, Fri & Sat, to 9pm Thu, 1-6pm
Sun; 🚇 all cross-city, 🚊 Jervis
Relive your childhood in this toy
superstore, with towering aisles
full of Barbies, Lego, V-Tech,
various action men, puzzles,
soft toys, board and electronic
games, and a whole room devoted to Playstations, Gameboys
and DVDs.

🖿 WINDING STAIR *Books*
☎ 873 3292; 40 Lower Ormond Quay;
🕑 9.30am-6pm Mon-Sat; 🚇 all cross-
city, 🚊 Jervis
There was a public outcry when
this creaky old place closed a
few years ago. It reopened its
doors and Dublin's bohemians,
students and literati once more
could thumb the fine selection of new and secondhand
books crammed into heaving
bookcases. When you've had

Toys for all the girls and boys at Smyths

enough of browsing, head up the
winding stairs to the excellent
restaurant (p116).

🍴 EAT
🍴 101 TALBOT
Mediterranean &
Middle Eastern   €€
☎ 874 5011; www.101talbot.com;
101 Talbot St; 🕑 5-11pm Tue-Sat;
🚇 all cross-city
Funky 101 Talbot is a perennial
favourite of artists, students, locals
and theatre-goers. They're attract-
ed by its eclectic menu, canteen-
style atmosphere and artwork. Its
scallops with black pudding and
raspberry dressing are divine.

WORTH THE TRIP: BEYOND THE ROYAL CANAL

Go north, past the Royal Canal, to discover not just a bunch of traditional suburbs but some of the more interesting sights and attractions of the city.

The high cathedral of Gaelic games, state-of-the-art **Croke Park** (☎ 836 3222; www .crokepark.ie; Clonliffe Rd, Dublin 3; ❤ Apr-Sep; ⊒ 3, 11, 11a, 16, 16a, 51a, 123) plays host to the most important matches of both the football and hurling championships, as well as all of Dublin's home games. Attached to the stadium, the **Croke Park Experience** (☎ 819 2323; http://museum.gaa.ie; general admission €5.50/4/3.50, museum & stadium tour €9.50/7/6; ❤ 9.30am-5pm Mon-Sat, noon-5pm Sun Apr-Oct, 10am-5pm Tue-Sat, noon-4pm Sun Nov-Mar) explores the history of hurling, Gaelic football, camogie (women's variant of hurling) and handball. Interactive screens let you test your skills, listen to recordings from special matches and replay historic moments. You can also tour the grounds and dressing rooms with a guide.

For something a little different, head northeast to the **Casino at Marino** (☎ 833 1618; www.heritageireland.ie; Malahide Rd, Marino; admission €3/1/2; ❤ 10am-6pm May-Sep, last tour 45min before closing; ⊒ 20a, 20b, 27, 27b, 42, 42c, 123, ⊒ Clontarf Rd), although you won't exactly be cashing in your chips here. Roman temple from the outside and kooky Georgian house inside, it is one of Ireland's finest – and weirdest – Palladian buildings. The house was built by Sir William Chambers for the eccentric James Caulfield (1728–99). While externally the building appears to contain just one room, the interior is a convoluted maze of chambers.

Further north, **Helix** (☎ 700 7000; www.thehelix.ie; Collins Ave, Glasnevin; ⊒ 4, 11, 13, 19), the beautifully designed arts centre at Dublin City University, has three venues hosting a range of shows, from music and theatre to ballet and opera.

🍴 BAR ITALIA *Italian* €€
☎ 874 1000; www.baritalia.ie; 28 Lower Ormond Quay; ❤ 10.30am-11pm Mon-Sat, 1-9pm Sun; ⊒ all cross-city; ♿ Ⓥ

One of a new generation of eateries that's showing the more established Italian restaurants how the Old Country *really* eats, Bar Italia's specialities are its rustic antipasto platters, ever-changing pasta dishes – perhaps tagliatelle with an Irish beef ragu – homemade risottos and excellent Palombini coffee.

🍴 BON GA *Korean* €€
☎ 872 7934; www.bonga.ie; 52 Capel St; ❤ 5.30pm-midnight; ⊒ all cross-city; Ⓥ

Korean barbecue is all well and – in this instance – very good, but there's something extra about this large, friendly place that is always buzzing with locals, visitors and immigrants alike: oh yeah, it's the karaoke rooms, where you can dine and sing to your heart's content. To get the vocal chords going try the *dongdong ju* rice wine or *soju,* basically a Korean vodka. Top night out.

Heading back towards the city, the suburb of Glasnevin is home to two historic sights that are perfect for a relaxed afternoon ramble. Recharge your batteries meandering arboretum trails and Victorian rose beds at the **National Botanic Gardens** (☎ 837 7596; Botanic Rd, Glasnevin; admission free; ⏱ 9am-6pm Mon-Sat, 11am-6pm Sun Apr-Oct, 10am-4.30pm Mon-Sat, 11am-4.30pm Sun Nov-Mar; 🚌 13, 19, 83), an important centre of horticultural and botanical study for more than 200 years, and home to more than 20,000 plant varieties spread over almost 20 hectares. Stretching west from the gardens, **Prospect Cemetery** (☎ 830 1133; www.glasnevin-cemetery.ie; Finglas Rd; admission free; ⏱ 24hr, tours 2.30pm Wed & Fri; 🚌 40, 40a) is Ireland's largest Catholic cemetery. It was established in 1832 and is a setting for part of *Ulysses*. A walk along its quiet pebbled paths among the huge yew trees and gothic tombs is about as creepy as it gets in daylight. The towers in the walls were used to watch for body snatchers working for the city's 19th-century surgeons. Steady your nerves afterwards in one of Dublin's most authentic traditional pubs, **Kavanagh's** (☎ 830 7978; 1 Prospect Sq, Glasnevin; ⏱ 10am-midnight), known locally as 'the Gravediggers'.

Another great way to spend a (warm) day is at the **National Aquatic Centre** (☎ 646 4300; www.nationalaquaticcentre.ie; Snugborough Rd, Blanchardstown; admission €14/12; ⏱ 6am-10pm Mon-Fri, 9am-8pm Sat & Sun; 🚌 38a from Hawkins St). Established in 2003 to accommodate the Special Olympics World Summer Games, this is the largest indoor water park in Europe. Besides its Olympic-size competition pool, it has fantastic water roller coasters, wave and surf machines, a leisure pool, and all types of flumes. Be prepared to join the shivering line of children queuing for slides on weekend afternoons.

🍽 **CHAPTER ONE** *French*   €€€
☎ 873 2266; www.chapteronerestaurant
.com; 18-19 Parnell Sq; ⏱ 12.30-2.30pm &
6-11pm Tue-Sat; 🚌 10, 11, 16, 19
Savour classic French cuisine in the
best restaurant north of the river,
in the lovely vaulted basement of
the Dublin Writers Museum (p107).
Getting a table here can take
months, which is what happens
when Monsieur Michelin bestows
one of his stars upon you. You'll
have to book in advance, but the
three-course pre-theatre special
(served before 7pm) is excellent.

🍽 **COBALT CAFÉ & GALLERY**
Cafe   €
☎ 873 0313; 16 N Great George's St;
⏱ 10am-4.30pm Mon-Fri; 🚌 all cross-
city; ♿ Ⓥ
This gorgeous, elegant cafe
housed in a bright and airy
Georgian drawing room is a must
if you're in the 'hood. Almost
opposite the James Joyce Centre,
the menu is simple but you'll relish
hearty soups by a roaring fire in
winter or bouncy fresh salads
and sandwiches in the garden on
warmer days.

🍴 LA TAVERNA DI BACCO

Italian €€

☎ 873 0040; 24 Lower Ormond Quay; 🕑 12.30-10.30pm Tue-Sat, from 5pm Sun; 🚌 all cross-city, 🚇 Jervis

Football-mad developer Mick Wallace has managed to single-handedly create a thriving new Italian quarter with cafes and eateries popping up all over Quartier Bloom, the new lane from Ormond Quay to Great Strand St. La Taverna (and, a few doors up, Enoteca Delle Langhe) serves simple pastas, antipasti and Italian cheeses, along with the delicious produce of his own vineyard and others in Piemonte.

🍴 MELODY *Chinese* €€

☎ 878 8988; 122 Capel St; 🕑 5.30pm-midnight; 🚌 all cross-city, 🚇 Jervis; Ⓥ

This busy restaurant might have been designed to suit the tastes of the city's Chinese community (lots of red lacquer and black marble), but it's popular with others, too, who come – often in big groups – for the decent grub and the warren of downstairs karaoke rooms.

🍴 SOUP DRAGON

Cafe & Soup €

☎ 872 3277; www.soupdragon.com; 168 Capel St; 🕑 8am-5.30pm Mon-Fri, 11am-5pm Sat; 🚌 all cross-city; 🚳 Ⓥ

Eat in or takeaway one of 12 tasty homemade soups, including Thai

green curry or fish chowder in full or low-fat options. Bowls come in three different sizes, and prices include homemade bread and a piece of fruit. Kick-start your day with the healthy all-day breakfast selection: fresh smoothies, generous bowls of yoghurt, fruit and muesli, or poached egg in a bagel.

🍴 WINDING STAIR

Modern Irish €€€

☎ 873 3292; www.winding-stair.com; 40 Lower Ormond Quay; 🕑 9am-6pm Mon-Sat, from 1pm Sun; 🚌 all cross-city, 🚇 Jervis

Housed within a beautiful Georgian building that was once home to the city's most beloved bookshop (the ground floor still is one, see p113), the conversion to elegant restaurant has been fault-less. The wonderful Irish menu – creamy fish pie, organic cabbage and bacon, steamed mussels, and Irish farmyard cheeses – coupled with an excellent wine list make for a memorable meal.

🍸 DRINK

🍸 CHURCH *Pub*

☎ 878 0223; Mary St; 🕑 10am-1am Mon-Wed, to 2.30am Thu-Sat, 12.30pm-midnight Sun; 🚇 Jervis

We don't normally go in for superpubs, but this one deserves a mention. Irish patriot Wolfe Tone, who was baptised here, and Arthur

Guinness, brewery founder, who married here, might have conflicting views on the fate of this remarkable early 18th-century church. The glorious restoration features an enormous organ and historically important wall plaques and inscriptions. Expect a well-heeled crowd.

⛶ FLOWING TIDE   *Pub*
☎ 874 0842; 9 Lower Abbey St;
🚌 all cross-city, 🚋 Abbey St
Directly opposite the Abbey Theatre, the Flowing Tide attracts a great mix of theatre-goers, no-bullshit northside locals and the odd thespian downing a quick one between rehearsals. It's loud, full of chat and a great place to drink. What more could you ask for in a pub?

⛶ SACKVILLE LOUNGE *Bar*
☎ 874 5222; Sackville Pl;
🚌 all cross-city, 🚋 Abbey St
This tiny 19th-century one-room, wood-panelled bar is discreetly located just off O'Connell St, which perhaps explains why it's so popular with actors, theatre-goers and anyone who appreciates a nice pint in a gorgeous old-style bar.

⛶ SIN É *Bar*
☎ 878 7009; 14-15 Upper Ormond Quay;
🚌 all cross-city, 🚋 Jervis
There's no real decor to speak of, but this place (pronounced *shin-ay*, meaning 'that's it' in Irish) buzzes almost nightly with a terrific mix of professionals and

Golden lighting, gleaming wood and a good pint at the Sackville Lounge

students, the uncool and the hip. It helps that the DJs are all uniformly excellent.

⭐ PLAY
⭐ ABBEY THEATRE
Performances
☎ 878 7222; www.abbeytheatre .ie; Lower Abbey St; admission Abbey Theatre €12-30, Peacock Theatre €12-25; ⏲ box office 10.30am-7pm Mon-Sat; 🚌 all cross-city, 🚉 Abbey St

It is scheduled to move to a purpose-built location in the Docklands, but for now Ireland's national theatre – including the smaller, experimental Peacock Theatre – still resides in a large concrete box by the river. It puts on new Irish works, as well as revivals of classic Irish plays by writers such as WB Yeats, JM Synge, Sean O'Casey, Brendan Behan and Samuel Beckett. See also p19.

⭐ AMBASSADOR THEATRE
Live Music
www.mcd.ie; Upper O'Connell St; ⏲ doors open 7.30pm; 🚌 all cross-city

This former cinema, at the top of O'Connell St, has thankfully kept much of its rococo interior intact. The view of its international acts on stage is better from the spacious downstairs auditorium, while on the mezzanine level it's seating only in old velvet cinema

seats, complete with drinks holders.

⭐ CINEWORLD *Cinema*
☎ 872 8400; www.cineworld.ie; Parnell Centre, Parnell St; ⏲ from10am; 🚌 all cross-city; ♿

The city centre's most modern cineplex has 17 screens showing all the latest releases.

⭐ GATE THEATRE *Performances*
☎ 874 4045; www.gate-theatre.ie; E Parnell Sq; admission €18-30; ⏲ box office 10am-7pm Mon-Sat; 🚌 all cross-city

International classics from the likes of Harold Pinter and Noel Coward, older Irish works by playwrights such as Oscar Wilde, George Bernard Shaw and Oliver Goldsmith, as well as newer plays are performed here. See also p19.

⭐ LAUGHTER LOUNGE
Comedy
☎ 1800 266 339; www.laughterlounge .ie; Eden Quay; admission €25-30; ⏲ shows start 9pm Thu-Sat; 🚌 all cross-city, 🚉 Abbey St

Dublin's only purpose-built comedy venue can squeeze 400 punters in for live shows, which feature four high-quality Irish and international acts each night. Admission includes entry to the post-comedy club, the After Lounge, with resident DJ.

Patrons in the bar area of Dublin's Gate Theatre

⭐ PANTI BAR
LGBT Entertainment

☎ 874 0710; www.pantibar.com;
Capel St; 🕐 4-11.30pm Sun-Wed, to
12.30am Thu-Sat; 🚌 37, 70, 134, 172,
🚆 Jervis

The northside's most outrageous
gay bar is almost always packed –
they come for the floor shows
both on and off the stage. Panti
offers a different theme every
night, from Monday night crafts to
Sunday night loungin' around.

⭐ TWISTED PEPPER
Club & Live Music

☎ 873 4800; www.bodytonicmusic.com;
54 Middle Abbey St; 🕐 8am-midnight
Mon-Wed, 10am-2.30am Thu-Sat;
🚌 all cross-city, 🚆 Abbey St

Dublin's coolest new venue comes
in four parts: the basement where
you can hear some of the best DJs
in town, the stage for live acts, the
secluded mezzanine bar area and
the cafe where you can get an Irish
breakfast all day.

>SMITHFIELD & PHOENIX PARK

An area very much in development, Smithfield promises to be cool and sophisticated, with new designer buildings surrounding a sexy square that will provide a meeting point for the trendy young things that shop, eat, drink and live nearby. It is happening, but it's not quite there. The main square, now the centrepiece of the new development, has been synonymous with markets since the 17th century and, in recent decades, was the scene of a bustling horse fair where deals were sealed with a spit in your hand. These are all gone now – hurriedly moved on because fruit 'n' veg and hoof inspections didn't fit the planned aesthetic. The 400,000-odd antique cobblestones that saw their share of horse manure over the decades were removed, hand-cleaned and re-laid alongside new granite slabs, giving the square a brand new look. Further on up the Liffey is Phoenix Park, the giant green lung that is the city's biggest playground.

SMITHFIELD & PHOENIX PARK

SEE

Dublin Zoo 1 A2
Four Courts 2 E4
National Museum of
   Ireland – Decorative
   Arts & History 3 D3
Old Jameson
   Distillery 4 E3
Phoenix Park 5 A2
St Michan's Church 6 E3

Y DRINK

Cobblestone 7 D3
Dice Bar 8 D4
Hughes' Bar 9 E3
Voodoo Lounge 10 D4

👁 SEE

👁 DUBLIN ZOO

☎ 677 1425; www.dublinzoo.ie; Phoenix Park; admission €15/10.50/43.50; 🕙 9.30am-6pm Mon-Sat, 10.30am-6pm Sun Mar-Sep, 9.30am-dusk Mon-Fri, 9.30am-dusk Sat, 10.30am-dusk Sun Oct-Feb; 🚌 10 from O'Connell St, 25 or 26 from Abbey St Middle; 🕭

The second-oldest public zoo in Europe, the Dublin Zoo calls itself home to more than 700 animals, including rhinos, gorillas, leopards, penguins and polar bears. Apart from the animal antics, children will enjoy the regular feedings, the minitrain ride through the zoo grounds, the African safari plains and, if all else fails, the big playground.

👁 FARMLEIGH

☎ 815 5900; www.farmleigh.ie; Phoenix Park, Castleknock; admission free; 🕙 10.30am-5.30pm Sat & Sun, may be closed for official events; 🚌 37 from city centre

Another splendid feather in architect James Gandon's cap, this fine Georgian-Victorian pile, once part of the Guinness estate, was restored to immaculate standard by the state in 2001. Only the ground floor, with a fantastic library and glass conservatory, is on view, but the vast pleasure gardens with lake, and walled and Japanese gardens are a delight to stroll. It is the apt setting for the RTE Summer Proms, a series of free popular classical concerts with guest conductors during July.

👁 FOUR COURTS

☎ 872 5555; Inns Quay; admission free; 🕙 9am-4.30pm Mon-Fri; 🚌 134, 🚆 Four Courts

With its 130m-long facade and neoclassical proportions, the Four Courts was built between 1786 and 1802 to the design of James Gandon. In 1922, the building was captured by anti-Treaty republicans, and pro-Treaty forces shelled the site to try to dislodge them. Displays on the building's history and reconstruction are on the 1st floor. Court hearings can be observed from public galleries between 10am and 4pm only.

👁 NATIONAL MUSEUM OF IRELAND – DECORATIVE ARTS & HISTORY

☎ 677 7444; www.museum.ie; Benburb St; admission free; 🕙 10am-5pm Tue-Sat, 2-5pm Sun; 🚌 25, 25a, 66, 67, 90, 92, 🚆 Museum; 🕭

Once the world's largest military barracks (named after Michael Collins), this splendid early neoclassical greystone building on the Liffey's northern banks is now home to the decorative arts and history collection of the National

Overlooked by the sombre Four Courts building, the Liffey glows an illuminated green

Museum of Ireland. Inside the imposing exterior lies a treasure trove of artefacts ranging from silver, ceramics and glassware to weaponry, furniture and folk-life displays – and an exquisite exhibition dedicated to iconic Irish designer Eileen Gray (1878–1976). Special events and educational workshops for kids are held regularly.

🌀 OLD JAMESON DISTILLERY
☎ 807 2355; www.jameson.ie; Bow St; admission €13.50/8/30; ⏱ tours every 35min 9am-5.30pm; 🚌 67, 67a, 68, 69, 79, 134, 🚆 Smithfield

Housed in the original Jameson distillery where the famous Irish whiskey was produced from 1791

to 1966, the museum tells the story of the site and the drink. A heavy dose of marketing is thrown in, but fans will enjoy the re-created old factory, detailed explanations of the distilling process and, of course, the free glass of Jameson at the end of the tour.

🌀 PHOENIX PARK
☎ 677 0095; www.phoenixpark.ie; park grounds free, visitor centre €2.75/1.25/7; ⏱ visitor centre 10am-6pm Apr-Sep, 10am-5pm Oct, 10am-5pm Mon-Sat Nov & Dec, 10am-5pm Sat & Sun Jan-Mar; 🚌 visitor centre 37, 38, 39, park gate 10, 25, 26, 66, 67 68, 69

One of the world's largest city parks is where you'll find MP3-rigged

MURDER IN THE PARK

In 1882, Lord Cavendish, British chief secretary for Ireland, and his assistant were stabbed to death in Phoenix Park by members of a Fenian splinter nationalist group called the Invincibles. The assassins escaped, but one of their comrades betrayed them and they were hanged at Kilmainham Gaol (p100).

joggers, grannies pushing buggies, ladies walking poodles, gardens, lakes, a sporting oval, and 300 deer. There are also cricket and polo grounds, a motor-racing track and some fine 18th-century residences, including those of the Irish president and the US ambassador. Free one hour tours of the president's residence depart the visitor centre on Saturday from 10.30am to 4.30pm.

ST MICHAN'S CHURCH

☎ 872 4154; Lower Church St; admission €4/3.50; ☷ 10am-12.45pm & 2-4.45pm Mon-Fri, 10am-12.45pm Sat May-Oct, 12.30-3.30pm Mon-Fri Nov-Apr; 🚌 134, 🚊 Four Courts

Founded by Danes in 1095, major rebuilding in 1686 and 1828 left little of the original structure. The church has a fine oak organ that may have been played by Handel, but the star attraction is the

Trying for a run during a Sunday cricket match in Phoenix Park

church's vault, where buried bodies have been gruesomely mummified by the magnesium limestone walls, limbs bursting out of coffins.

☿ DRINK

☿ COBBLESTONE
Trad Music Pub

☎ 872 1799; 77 N King St; admission €8-12; 🚌 134, 🚇 Smithfield

Bordering Smithfield Sq, this great old spit-on-the-floor bar is Pixies' Frank Black's favourite hangout when he's in town. A great bunch of rising stars and tried-and-tested old hands of the trad scene play sessions here nightly till everyone's turfed out the door.

☿ DICE BAR *Bar*

☎ 674 6710; 79 Queen St; 🚌 25, 37, 39, 79, 90, 🚇 Smithfield

Co-owned by singer Huey from the Fun Lovin' Criminals, the Dice Bar looks like something you'd expect to find on New York's Lower East Side. Its black-and-red painted interior and dripping candles make it a magnet for Dublin's beautiful beatnik crowds. Pull up in your Thunderbird for Teddy Boy rockabilly night on Sunday.

☿ HUGHES' BAR *Trad Music Pub*

☎ 872 6540; 19 Chancery St; 🚌 all cross-city, 🚇 Four Courts

By day this pub is popular with barristers and their clients from

Voodoo Lounge – known for its decadent decor

the nearby Four Courts, and the early opening hours cater for the workers from the market across the street. But by night the place transforms into a traditional music venue, where you'll hear some skilled session players put their instruments to work.

☿ VOODOO LOUNGE *Bar*

☎ 873 6013; 37 Arran Quay; ☽ 12.30-11.30pm Mon-Wed, to 2.30am Thu-Sat, to 11pm Sun; 🚌 25, 37, 39, 79, 90, 🚇 Smithfield

Run by the same crew as Dice Bar (left), Voodoo Lounge, on the quays just south of Smithfield, is a long, dark bar with decadent, Gothic Louisiana–style decor. Indie, electropop and rock music are played loud, and that's the way the fun-lovin' crowd likes it.

>BEYOND THE GRAND CANAL

Dublin's wealthiest suburbs are laid out south of the Grand Canal, which marks the city centre's southern boundary. These include the much-sought-after postcode of Dublin 4, a byword for posh sophistication and privilege that everyone not from there likes to envy and poke fun at – in Dublin envy and comedy make for comfortable bedfellows. As you explore the suburbs, you'll quickly notice there's plenty to be green about, and lots to see and do too, from buying upmarket organic fare to attending a trad session or having a flutter on the dogs.

Built to connect Dublin with the River Shannon in the centre of Ireland, the Grand Canal makes a graceful 6km loop around south Dublin and enters the Liffey at Ringsend, through locks that were built in 1796. The large Grand Canal Dock, flanked by Hanover and Charlotte Quays, is now used by windsurfers and canoeists and is the site of major new development.

BEYOND THE GRAND CANAL

◉ SEE			⑪ EAT			★ PLAY		
Dillon Garden	1	C4	Expresso Bar	3	D2	Royal Dublin Society		
Herbert Park	2	D3	French Paradox	4	D3	Concert Hall	7	E3
			Itsa4	5	F3	Shelbourne Greyhound		
			Juniors	6	D2	Stadium	8	E1

👁 SEE

📷 AIRFIELD TRUST GARDENS

☎ 298 4301; www.airfield.ie; Upper Kilmacud Rd, Dundrum; admission €6/3/18; 🕓 10am-4pm Tue-Sat, 11am-4pm Sun; 🚌 44, 46a, 48a; ♿

Once the home of eccentric philanthropist sisters Letitia and Naomi Overend, the Airfield estate is now held in trust for public use. Though the house is closed to the public (except for the excellent cafe), the

True Dubliners, it is said, are born within the confines of the two canals, the Grand and Royal, that encircle the inner city. Thanks to the vision of the Wide Street Commission who, nearly a quarter of a century ago, restricted building closer than 32m to the water, the tree-lined canal paths have become an amenity enjoyed by Dubliners. An evening barge trip is an atmospheric way to experience the canals. Board **La Peniche** (☎ 087 790 0077; www.lapeniche.ie; Grand Canal, Mespil Rd; 🕓 8.30-10.30pm Thu), sit on deck and enjoy fine wine and food while your skipper navigates the locks.

lovely 16-hectare grounds with walled gardens, pet farm, vintage car museum and medicinal garden are great for a stroll.

📷 DILLON GARDEN

☎ 497 1308; www.dillongarden.com; 45 Sandford Rd, Ranelagh; admission €5; 🕓 2-6pm Mar, Jul & Aug, 2-6pm Sun Apr-Jun & Sep; 🚌 11, 13, 🚉 Beechwood

Gardening enthusiasts will enjoy a visit to award-winning gardener Helen Dillon's own dramatic garden at her 1830s home. Inspired by Granada's Alhambra, the walled garden is inventively landscaped with an impressive canal feature and colour-coded exotic borders. Children are not admitted.

Gently boating down the Grand Canal

Time for a break and some sunshine on a patch of green alongside the Grand Canal

HERBERT PARK

Ballsbridge; admission free;
dawn-dusk; 5, 7, 7a, 8, 45, 46,
Sandymount, Lansdowne Rd
A gorgeous swathe of green
lawns, ponds and flower beds
near the Royal Dublin Society
Showgrounds. Sandwiched between prosperous Ballsbridge and
Donnybrook, the park runs along
the River Dodder. There are tennis
courts and a kids' playground
here, too.

JAMES JOYCE MUSEUM

280 9265; Martello tower,
Sandycove; admission €7.50/6.30;
10am-1pm & 2-5pm Mon-Sat, 2-6pm
Sun Apr-Oct, by arrangement only
Nov-Mar; 59 from Dun Laoghaire,
Sandycove, Glasthule
Strikingly located in a Martello
tower overlooking Dublin Bay
in the salubrious seaside suburb
of Sandycove, the James Joyce
Museum's contents combine

FORTY FOOT SWIM

Just below the James Joyce Museum's Martello tower is the Forty Foot Pool. At the close of the first chapter of *Ulysses*, Buck Mulligan heads to the pool for a morning swim, an activity which is still a local tradition. For years the spot was reserved for male-only nude bathing, but women are now allowed. Though a sign warns that 'trunks must be worn', die-hard men still keep the tradition up before 9am.

memorabilia from the celebrated writer's life with a dramatic setting that has a story all its own. The opening scene of *Ulysses* is set on the tower's roof. Visit on Bloomsday (16 June) for special events.

🌳 MARLAY HOUSE & PARK

Grange Rd, Rathfarnham; admission free; 🕐 10am-dusk; 🚌 15c, 16, 16a, 48; ♿

Marlay Park, 9km south of the city centre, is a wonderful 83-hectare open space, with 17th-century buildings, wooded areas, duck ponds, abundant wildlife, a walled garden, sculpture trail and craft centre. Kids will especially love the fairy bridge, massive playground, BMX cycle track, skateboard park and, in summer, the minitrain (3pm to 5pm May to September) that jostles around a field track.

🛍 SHOP

🛍 BLACKROCK MARKET
Market

Main St, Blackrock; 🕐 11am-5.30pm Sat, from 10am Sun; 🚊 Blackrock

The long-running and charmingly atmospheric Blackrock Market tumbles out of an old merchant house and yard in this seaside village. It has all manner of stalls selling everything from New Age crystals and dodgy Dollar albums to futons and piping-hot French waffles.

🛍 PEOPLE'S PARK MARKET
Gourmet Food

☎ 087 957 3647; People's Park, Dun Laoghaire; 🕐 11am-4pm Sun; 🚌 11, 11a, 13b, 🚊 Dun Laoghaire

Organic meat and veg, local seafood, Irish fruit and farm cheeses are the mainstay at this popular market in the south Dublin suburb of Dun Laoghaire. Grab a burger and sit on the lawn.

🍴 EAT

🍴 EXPRESSO BAR
Mediterranean €€€

☎ 660 0585; 1 St Mary's Rd; 🕐 7.30am-9.15pm Mon-Fri, 9am-9.15pm Sat & 10am-5pm Sun; 🚌 10; ♿

Hidden away on a leafy suburban road off Upper Baggot St, this hip, minimalist place with leather seating and subdued lighting attracts local rock stars and other types normally seen only in the social columns. Top nosh such as lamb shank, grilled balsamic chicken or baked sea bass with lime and mint potatoes should keep most folk happy when they're not people-watching over *Hello!* magazine.

🍴 FRENCH PARADOX
French   €€
☎ 660 4068; www.thefrenchparadox
.com; 53 Shelbourne Rd; ◷ noon-3pm & 5-10pm Mon-Sat, noon-4pm Sun; 🚌 5, 7, 7a, 8, 45, 46

This bright and airy wine bar over an excellent wine shop of the same name serves fine authentic French dishes such as cassoulet, a variety of foie gras, cheese and charcuterie plates, and large green salads. All there to complement the main attraction:

a dazzling array of fine wines, mostly French unsurprisingly, sold by the bottle, glass or even 6.25cL taste! A little slice of Paris in Dublin.

🍴 ITSA4 *Modern Irish*   €€
☎ 219 4676; www.itsabagel.com; 6a Sandymount Green; ◷ noon-2pm & 6-9pm Tue-Fri, from 11am Sat, noon-8pm Sun; 🚊 Sandymount; 🚼 Ⓥ

While Itsa4's funky flamboyant interior has been used for many fashion shoots, organic chef and writer Domini Kemp is far from frivolous. Her latest venture continues her ambitions to deliver well-sourced, quality food in deli-cious, down-to-earth ways. Lamb shank with lyonnaise potatoes or chicory, blue cheese and glazed pear salad are incredible. Serious food for fun people.

Handsome Dalkey lies about 13km south of the city centre, a trendy and desirable village full of pubs, restaurants and – increasingly – Dublin's well-to-do.

The roofless **Archibald's Castle** on Castle St is closed except at Christmas, when a nativity crib is open to visitors. Across the road is the 15th-century **Dalkey Castle Heritage Centre**, which houses an interesting **visitor centre** (☎ 285 8366; admission €6/4/16; ◷ 9.30am-5pm Mon-Fri, from 11am Sat & Sun). Exhibits explain the castle's defence systems, the history of the area's transport and various myths and legends. The Living History tour at weekends includes a re-enactment of medieval Dublin. The remains of the 11th-century **St Begnet's church & graveyard** are also here.

The waters around **Dalkey Island** are popular with scuba divers – catch one of the small boats touting for business at Coliemore Harbour. To get to Dalkey from Dublin, catch the DART (see p160).

Studying the doggy form guide at the Shelbourne Greyhound Stadium

🍴 **JUNIORS** *Modern Irish* €€
☎ 664 3648; www.juniors.ie; 2 Bath
Ave, Sandymount; 🕐 12.30-11.30pm;
🚌 5, 7, 7a, 8, 45, 46, 🚉 Lansdowne Rd
Cramped and easily mistaken for
any old cafe, Juniors is anything
but ordinary – the food (mostly
Irish dishes, with all locally sourced
produce) is delicious, the atmosphere always buzzing (it's often
hard to get a table) and the ethos

top-notch, which is down to the
two brothers who run the place.

⭐ PLAY
⭐ **COMHALTAS CEOLTÓIRÍ
ÉIREANN** *Live Music*
☎ 280 0295; www.comhaltas.com; 35
Belgrave Sq, Monkstown; show or céilidh
€10; 🕐 9pm-midnight Mon-Sat; 🚌 7,
7a, 8 from Trinity College, 🚉 Seapoint

Serious aficionados of traditional music should make the trip here. The name (col-tas kyohl-thory erin) means 'Fraternity of Traditional Musicians of Ireland'. Here you'll find the best Irish music and dancing in Dublin, with some of the country's top players. There are nightly shows, but the 'craic is mighty' at Friday night's céilidh (group Irish dance). See also p22.

★ **ROYAL DUBLIN SOCIETY CONCERT HALL** *Performances*
☎ 668 0866; www.rds.ie; Ballsbridge; 🚌 5, 7, 7a, 8, 45, 🚉 Sandymount; ♿
The huge concert hall at the RDS Showgrounds hosts a rich, varied program of classical music and opera throughout the year, with Irish and international performers.

★ **SHELBOURNE GREYHOUND STADIUM** *Sporting Venues*
☎ 668 3502; www.shelbournepark.com; S Lotts Rd; admission €12; 🕐 7-10.30pm Wed, Thu & Sat; 🚌 3, 7, 7A, 8, 45 & 84 from Trinity College
All the comforts, including a restaurant overlooking the track, make going to the dogs one of the best nights out around. Table service (including betting) means that you don't even have to get out of your seat. See also p21.

>SNAPSHOTS

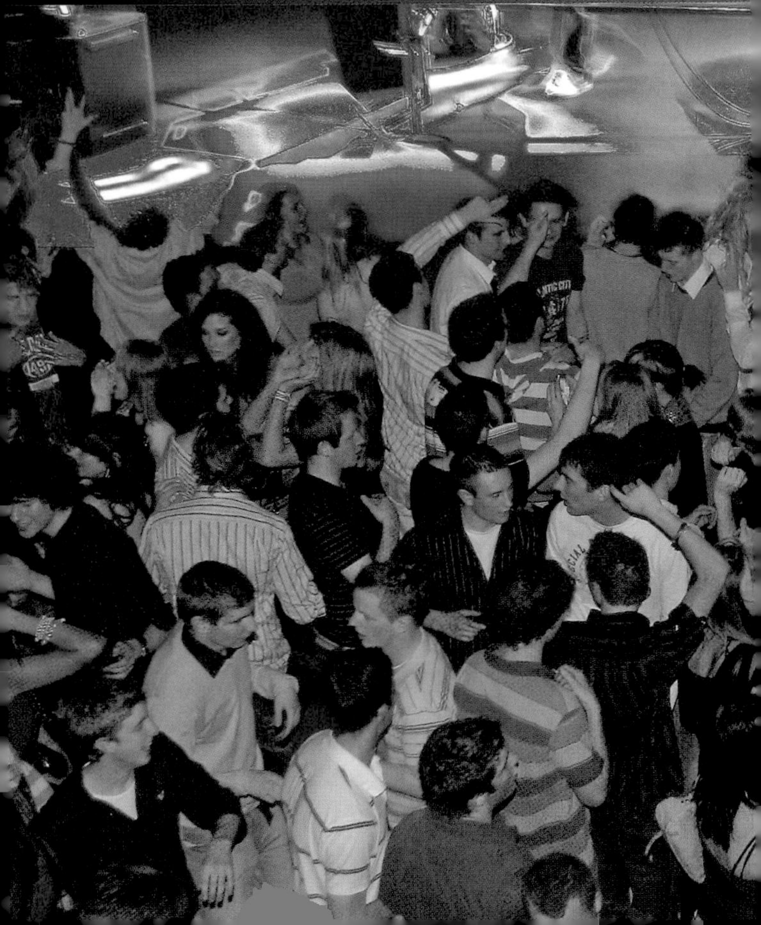

Whatever your passion or poison – toe-tapping at traditional music gigs; getting to grips with the ferocity of Gaelic football; or indulging in the greatest of Dublin pastimes, socialising at the pub – there's plenty to do in the capital and much more besides. It's all about making the right choices!

> Accommodation	136
> Drinking	138
> Kids	140
> Architecture	141
> Clubbing	142
> Food	143
> Gaelic Football	144
> Gardens & Parks	145
> Gay & Lesbian	146
> James Joyce	147
> Music	148
> Shopping	149
> Theatre	150

Dancing up an aquamarine-lit storm at Tripod (p94)

ACCOMMODATION

Over the last decade Dublin's beds have been transformed from lumpy to luxuriant, as hoteliers and B&B owners gave their properties a serious going-over to meet the demands of the tourist tsunami that made Dublin one of Europe's most visited capitals.

With the death of the Celtic Tiger, however, and the dip in tourist numbers, the new buzzword is 'value'. Hoteliers have responded with cheaper beds as they seek to guarantee the future of their properties. With so many deals now on offer room rates can vary wildly from day to day, never mind season to season – always check online and query the rack rate.

Dublin gets busy in summer and it can be tough to get a central bed from May to September. By 'central' we mean the area roughly between the top of O'Connell St and the bottom of Camden St, stretching along the Docklands to the east. There's very little west of the two cathedrals save a couple of hostels and a pair of midrange chain hotels in Kilmainham.

Within this relatively small area there are large differences, and the south-north divide remains a constant: you're more likely to get better value for money north of the Liffey. A large room in a comfortable B&B in the northside suburbs will cost you less than a shoebox-sized room in a mediocre guesthouse within walking distance of Grafton St, but here it's all about location – in this case right in the heart of the action.

If you're looking for something with a little more character, you should consider the leafy suburbs of Ballsbridge, Donnybrook or Ranelagh immediately south of the city centre, which are pretty accessible by public transportation or cab (if you don't fancy a 30-minute walk).

---

lonely planet Hotels & Hostels

Need a place to stay? Find and book it at lonelyplanet.com. More than 55 properties are featured for Dublin – each personally visited, thoroughly reviewed and happily recommended by a Lonely Planet author. From hostels to high-end hotels, we've hunted out the places that will bring you unique and special experiences. Read independent reviews by authors and other travel aficionados like you, and get practical information including amenities, maps and photos. Then reserve your room simply and securely via Haystack – our online booking service. It's all at www.lonelyplanet.com/accommodation.

Nearly all properties include breakfast in their rate, which invariably includes the option of the heart-stoppingly delicious Irish fry.

If you arrive without accommodation, staff at Dublin Tourism's walk-in booking offices (p165) will find you a room for €4.50 (€7.50 for self-catering accommodation) plus a 10% deposit.

WEB RESOURCES

Internet bookings made in advance are your best bet for deals on accommodation. Try **Gulliver Info Res** (www.gulliver.ie), **Dublin Tourism** (www.visitdublin.com) or book direct from your chosen accommodation's own website.

Other services that can get you a room at a competitive rate include **All Dublin Hotels** (www.all-dublin-hotels.com), **Dublin City Centre Hotels** (www.dublin.city-centre -hotels.com), **Dublin Hotels** (www.dublinhotels.com) and **Hostel Dublin** (www.hosteldublin.com).

Self-catering apartments are a good option for visitors staying a few days, groups of friends, or families with kids. Apartments range from one-room studios to two-bed flats with lounge areas, and include bathrooms and kitchenettes. Try:

Clarion Stephen's Hall (www.premgroup.com)
Home From Home Apartments (www.yourhomefromhome.com)
Latchfords (www.latchfords.ie)
Oliver St John Gogarty's Penthouse Apartments (www.gogartys.ie)

MOST STYLISH MIDRANGE SLEEPS
> Ariel House (www.ariel-house.net)
> Number 31 (www.number31.ie)
> Trinity Lodge (www.trinitylodge.com)
> Irish Landmark Trust (www.irish landmark.com)
> Pembroke Townhouse (www.pem broketownhouse.ie)

BEST VALUE FOR MONEY
> Trinity College (www.tcd.ie)
> Merrion Hall (www.halpinsprivate hotels.com)
> Waterloo House (www.waterloohouse.ie)
> Aberdeen Lodge (www.halpinsprivate hotels.com)
> Isaac's Hostel (www.isaacs.ie)

BEST DESIGNER HOTELS
> Dylan (www.dylan.ie)
> Clarence Hotel (www.theclarence.ie)
> Bentleys (www.brownesdublin.com)
> Morrison (www.morrisonhotel.ie)
> Morgan Hotel (www.themorgan.com)

BEST HOTEL BARS TO PRETEND YOU'RE A GUEST IN
> Radisson Blu Royal Hotel (www .radissonblu.ie/royalhotel-dublin)
> Merrion (www.merrionhotel.com)
> Shelbourne (www.theshelbourne.ie)
> Four Seasons (www.fourseasons .com/dublin)
> Westbury (www.doylecollection.com)

DRINKING

It's like getting bumped on the streets of New York or being the victim of haughty rudeness in Paris: you cannot fully experience Dublin without spending at least some of your time here in a pub. And with nearly 900 to choose from, it's difficult to be disappointed, as no matter where you are in the city centre you can find a decent boozer to observe – and preferably participate in – the raucous conversations, the philosophical observations that only make sense after a couple of drinks, the joke-telling competitions, the impromptu and often atonal singalongs…and the beer: the pints of black velvet beauty adorned with the Guinness harp. For no matter how sophisticated and cosmopolitan Dublin has become, the pub remains the alpha and omega of all Dublin social life. You will *never* understand this city or its people if you don't cross the pub's welcoming threshold at least once, and settle in for a night whose outcome you shouldn't even try to predict.

Needless to say, pubs are invariably always busy, especially around touristy Temple Bar, where authenticity has been largely sacrificed for unadulterated fun. There are many busy, sociable and traditional bars on either side of Grafton St. Wexford/Camden St in SoDa is the new corridor of cool, although Dawson St, which it replaced, is still putting up a fight, while the quays, for so long the poster-child for grim old Dublin, have some terrific spots worth checking out. Georgian Dublin has a good mix of pubs, most of which fill up with office workers after hours (although that's not as unattractive a proposition as it might sound elsewhere).

There's no such thing as the *best* pub in town, nor should there be: everyone has their favourites, but most people agree on the elements that make up a great pub – warm ambience, good service and a decent pint. And when Dubliners talk about a 'decent pint' they are referring exclusively to Guinness, the pouring of which is still considered a craft by the city's aficionados. We urge you to try one, particularly in the likes of Mulligan's (p73), Grogan's Castle Lounge (p93) or the Sackville Lounge (p117), all of which have a reputation for serving a fine pint.

From Monday to Thursday pubs stop serving at 11.30pm, on Friday and Saturday it's 12.30am, and Sunday 11pm, with half an hour's drink-up time each night. Several city-centre bars have late licences. For the latest on the city's pubs, check out www.dublinpubs.ie.

TOP FIVE PUBS FOR...
> A decent pint and a chat – Grogan's Castle Lounge (p93)
> Beats and beatniks – Anseo (p91)
> To be seen in scene – Bar With No Name (p91)
> Fiddles and bodhráns – Cobblestone (p125)
> Tasty tapas – Market Bar (p93)

TOP DJ BARS
> Bernard Shaw (p91)
> Dice Bar (p125)
> Village (p95)
> Twisted Pepper (p119)
> Sín É (p117)

LANDMARK PUBS
> Oldest – Brazen Head (p103)
> Most famous owners (U2) – Octagon Bar (p73)

GOING SOLO
> Kehoe's (p50)
> Globe (p93)
> Mulligan's (p73)
> Solas (p93)
> Toner's (p63)

Top left Known for its tapas, SoDa's Market Bar (p93) is a welcoming place for a casual pint

KIDS

Dublin is a reasonably child-friendly city, but poor transport means lots of walking and there are few public spots to stop and rest (particularly on the northside). Bear in mind that under-16s are banned from pubs after 7pm – even if they're accompanied by their parents – but the plus side is that under-fives travel free on all public transport and most admission prices have an under-16s reduced fee.

There's also a dearth of public toilets in the city centre, although the major shopping centres have toilets and baby-change facilities. Although breast-feeding in Dublin is not an especially common sight (Ireland has one of the lowest rates of it in the world), you can do so with impunity pretty much anywhere and you won't get so much as a stare.

Many hotels in Dublin provide babysitting services (normally €10 to €12 per hour) or, though more expensive, you could try a couple of agencies who provide professional nannies. It's up to you to negotiate a fee with the nanny but €13 to €18 per hour is the average, plus taxi fare. Agencies include **Belgrave Agency** (☎ 280 9341; 55 Mulgrave St, Dun Laoghaire; per hr €15 plus 21.5% VAT) and **Babysitters Ireland** (www.babysitters.ie; 7a Sweetman Ave, Blackrock; per hr €12-17).

For some great children's workshops and exhibitions check out the **Ark** (☎ 670 7788; www.ark.ie; 11a Eustace St; admission varies; ☼ activity times vary), a cultural centre for kids.

TOP SIGHTS FOR KIDS
> Airfield Trust Gardens (p128)
> Dublin Zoo (p122)
> Dublinia (p98)
> Marlay House and Park (p130)
> National Aquatic Centre (p115)

TOP W'END & HOLIDAY PROGRAMS
> Dublin City Gallery, Hugh Lane (p106)
> Irish Museum of Modern Art (p99, pictured above)
> National Gallery of Ireland (p55)
> National Museum (p56)
> Temple Bar Diversions Festival (p25)

ARCHITECTURE

With one incredible exception and a handful of new efforts, Dublin doesn't really have a lot of architectural kudos. Too much urban planning by tasteless, myopic and greedy developers is the usual excuse, and we'll stick to it, too. The big exception, of course, is Dublin's Georgian heritage, visible in not just the fine residences and public buildings but the wide roads, gardens and elegant squares that were laid out from roughly 1780 to 1830.

The 20th century was especially unkind to Dublin – buildings of note include Busáras (Map p105, F3), the International Modernist bus station designed by Michael Scott in the 1940s, and Paul Koralek's 1967 Berkeley Library at Trinity (Map p39, D2) – but the dawn of the 21st has been quite a bit brighter, especially in the development of the docklands.

The snazzy new National Convention Centre (off Map p105), designed by Kevin Roche, is perhaps the most eye-catching new building in the docklands, but equally impressive is Daniel Libeskind's stunning Grand Canal Theatre overlooking Grand Canal Dock (Map p127, D1). A couple of new bridges spanning the Liffey are also worth noting, especially Santiago Calatrava's latest offering, the Samuel Beckett Bridge (off Map p105) spanning the Liffey between Sir John Rogerson's Quay and Guild St.

Reflecting City (www.reflectingcity.com) offers virtual tours of all the major urban renewal areas, while **Archéire** (www.irish-architecture.com) is a comprehensive site covering all things to do with Irish architecture and design.

BEST OF GEORGIAN
> Custom House (p106)
> Four Courts (p122)
> Leinster House (p55)
> Powerscourt Centre (p44)
> Newman House (p57)

BEST BRIDGES
> Ha'penny (Map p65, D1)
> Samuel Beckett (off Map p105)
> James Joyce (Map p97, D1, pictured)
> O'Connell (Map p65, F1)
> Millennium (Map p65, C2)

CLUBBING

Not quite the clubbers' paradise that it was for a brief, crazy and e-fuelled moment in the late 1990s, Dublin's clubbing scene tends to huddle around the safe middle ground. Still, there's no lack of choice if you want to dance (part of) the night away. The spread of late-night bars advertising loud music and booze without an admission fee have certainly dented the clubs' monopoly on late-night fun, but then again 'late night' is a relative term: party-pooping opening hours – with their 2.30am finishing-up times – will shock all but British visitors. But, misery loves company, and you'll be among tens of thousands as you stumble into the night looking for a ride home.

Everybody seems to flock to Temple Bar, where you'll find at least one terrific club. Celebrity spotters should hit the clubs around Grafton St, but we think SoDa is your best for just good old-fashioned dancing – from Rí Rá (p94) to the Tripod (p94) you'll find a handful of clubs to suit your needs, whether it be chart-toppers or the dirtiest electro beats. North of the Liffey, Abbey St is home to the new kid on the block, Twisted Pepper (p119), which is one of the best in the city.

Check out the free weekly *Event Guide* for listings or go online at www.dublinks.com.

TOP FIVE CLUBS
> Rí Rá (p94)
> PoD (p94)
> Twisted Pepper (p119)
> Think Tank (p77)
> Button Factory (p75)

TOP FIVE DJS TO LOOK OUT FOR
> Arveene
> Billy Scurry
> Bodytonic Crew
> Mo Kelly
> Johnny Moy

TOP FIVE CLUB NIGHTS
> Pogo (Twisted Pepper, p119; 🗓 Fri)
> Strictly Handbag (Sugar Club; p63; 🗓 Fri)
> Antics (PoD, p94; 🗓 Sat)
> Transmission (Button Factory, p75; 🗓 Sat)
> Sundays (Ukiyo; p91; 🗓 Sun)

TOP CLUBS TO DRESS UP FOR
> Lillie's Bordello (p51)
> Renard's (p63)
> Rí Rá (p94)

FOOD

Good news for foodies visiting Dublin: the market is changing, and for the better. Restaurateurs have finally twigged to the idea that not every meal has to be a once-a-year splurge and that wallet-friendly menus mean more bankable turnover. They're happy and we're happy. All over Dublin, thankfully, midpriced restaurants are cropping up that offer very good food at competitive prices.

You can still eat French (and Irish) haute cuisine any night of the week, but you'll also find Korean, Nepalese, Brazilian and pretty much everything in between.

The most concentrated restaurant area is Temple Bar, but apart from a handful of good places, the bulk of eateries offer unimaginative fodder and cheap set menus for tourists. Better food and service can usually be found on either side of Grafton St, while the top-end restaurants are clustered around Merrion Sq and Fitzwilliam Sq. Fast-food chains dominate the northside, though some fine eateries are finally appearing there, too.

Ireland has excellent beef, pork, seafood, dairy foods and winter vegetables, and many good restaurants now source their ingredients locally, from organic and artisan producers.

For many restaurants, particularly those in the centre, it's worth booking for Friday or Saturday nights to ensure a table.

TOP FIVE FOOD FAVES
> Best brunch – Odessa (p90)
> Best sandwich to go – Bottega Toffoli (p86)
> Best informal grub – Honest to Goodness (p88)
> Best lunch – Gruel (p71)
> Best splurge – Patrick Guilbaud (p61)

TOP FIVE FOR LOCAL PRODUCE
> Green Nineteen (p88)
> Juniors (p132)
> L'Ecrivain (p61)
> People's Park Market (p130)
> Temple Bar Farmers Market (p69)

SNAPSHOTS

GAELIC FOOTBALL

Hurling and football (not to be confused with Association Football, the *other* game) are the main sports of the **Gaelic Athletic Association** (www.gaa.ie), and have a massive national following. Hurling is the more elegant sport, but in Dublin it's all about football, where a round ball is kicked along the ground soccer-style, or passed between players as in rugby. If you want a genuinely enthralling experience, try to get to Croke Park (p114, pictured below) to watch the Dublin county team play in the All Ireland Championship, which runs roughly from April to the third Sunday in September.

The Dubs – who play in two tones of blue – are a traditional power-house of the game, having won the championship 22 times, second only to their great rivals, Kerry. Their fans are best described as boisterous: when they're not singing 'Molly Malone' or 'Dublin in the Rare Auld Times' they can be heard letting the opposition know exactly what they think of them.

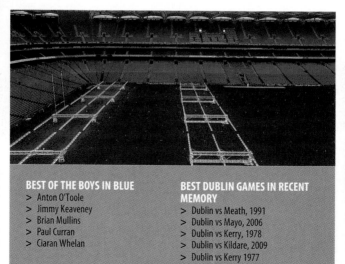

BEST OF THE BOYS IN BLUE
> Anton O'Toole
> Jimmy Keaveney
> Brian Mullins
> Paul Curran
> Ciaran Whelan

BEST DUBLIN GAMES IN RECENT MEMORY
> Dublin vs Meath, 1991
> Dublin vs Mayo, 2006
> Dublin vs Kerry, 1978
> Dublin vs Kildare, 2009
> Dublin vs Kerry 1977

GARDENS & PARKS

Not only does Dublin have a handful of the most beautifully manicured Georgian parks in Europe, but it is also home to the world's largest – wait for it – enclosed, nonwildlife, city park in the world. Despite the qualifiers, Phoenix Park (p123) – all 709 magnificent hectares of it – is larger than *all* of the major London parks…put together. Fallow deer, a zoo, sports grounds aplenty, the president's gaff, what more could one want?

Not nearly as big, but impressive for a host of other reasons, are Dublin's Georgian squares. St Stephen's Green (p58, pictured below) is the city's most frequented – on a summer's day you can barely find a spot of green to lay your head on, for the numbers sprawled out on its beautifully kept lawns. Merrion Sq (p55) is probably more gorgeous still and Fitzwilliam Sq (p54) is small but perfectly proportioned, but our favourite spot of all is the relatively unknown Iveagh Gardens (p54), a stone's throw from St Stephen's Green, but miles away in terms of tranquillity and peace.

TOP FIVE GREEN ACTIVITIES
> A summer cricket match at Trinity College
> Feeding the ducks in St Stephen's Green
> A lunchtime summer's gig at the bandstand, St Stephen's Green
> Reading the witty commentary on the Oscar Wilde Statue, Merrion Sq
> Polo – the one with horses – in Phoenix Park

TOP FIVE SPOTS FOR A ROMANTIC LIAISON
> The rocks in St Stephen's Green
> The secluded middle of Merrion Sq
> At the back of the Iveagh Gardens
> By the polo grounds in Phoenix Park – but during the day only!
> Anywhere in Fitzwilliam Sq

GAY & LESBIAN

Dublin's not a bad place to be gay. Most people wouldn't bat an eyelid at public displays of affection between same-sex couples, or cross-dressing in the city centre, but discretion is advised in the suburbs. If you are harassed on the streets don't hesitate to call the **Gay and Lesbian Garda Liaison Officer** (☎ 666 9000) or the **Sexual Assault Unit** (☎ 666 6000, Pearse St Garda Station).

There is a range of useful organisations, publications and online resources for LGBT travellers:

Gay Switchboard Dublin (☎ 872 1055; www.gayswitchboard.ie; ☿ 7.30am-9.30pm Mon-Fri, 3.30-6pm Sat) A friendly and useful voluntary service that can advise on everything from finding accommodation to legal issues.

National Lesbian and Gay Federation (NLGF; ☎ 671 9076; 2 Scarlet Row, Temple Bar) Publishes *Gay Community News* (www.gcn.ie), a free news- and issues-based monthly paper.

Outhouse (☎ 873 4932; www.outhouse.ie; 105 Capel St) Gay, lesbian and bisexual resource centre. Great stop-off point to see what's on, check noticeboards and meet people. It publishes the free Ireland's *Pink Pages*, a directory of gay-centric services, which is also accessible on the website.

BEST GAY & LESBIAN FESTIVALS & EVENTS
> Mardi Gras (p25)
> International Dublin Gay Theatre Festival (p25)
> Lesbian and Gay Film Festival (www .gaze.ie)

TOP GAY NIGHTS
> Dolly Does Dragon (Dragon, p92, ☿ Mon)
> Space 'N' Veda (George, p92, ☿ Wed)
> Panti Show (Panti Bar, p119, ☿ Thu)
> Bingo (George, p92, ☿ Sun)

JAMES JOYCE

The Greatest Irish Writer of All Time. Not bad for a guy whose literary output included two books so challenging *(Ulysses* and the virtually impossible *Finnegans Wake)* that most people have never even tried to read them. No matter. James Joyce is deserving of his title (if not the Nobel Prize that eluded him) by virtue of the simply magnificent *Dubliners,* a collection of short stories that every visitor to Dublin should read, for they paint as intimate and as accurate a portrait of the city's character today as when Joyce wrote them 100 years ago.

Never mind that for most of his life and for some years thereafter Joyce was treated by Irish authorities as a literary pornographer: today, in a more enlightened era, Joyce is the city's foremost literary genius, so the tourist office makes a big deal of Bloomsday and any other Joyce-related tidbits.

On 16 June each year, Joyce-lovers take to the streets in a re-enactment of Leopold Bloom's journey around Dublin in *Ulysses.* You can don Edwardian gear and join in on the Bloomsday fun (p25), which involves readings, dramatisations and feasting on Gorgonzola cheese and glasses of Burgundy. Points of activity include the James Joyce Museum at Sandycove (p129), where *Ulysses* begins, Sweny's Chemist (Map p39, F2), Davy Byrne's pub (Map p39, C3) and the National Library (p56).

TOP FIVE JOYCE LANDMARKS
> James Joyce House of the Dead (p100)
> Leopold & Molly Bloom's House (Map p121, F1)
> Davy Byrne's (Map p39, C3)
> James Joyce Cultural Centre (p108)
> James Joyce Museum (p129)

TOP FIVE JOYCE QUOTES
> A man's errors are his portals of discovery.
> Christopher Columbus, as everyone knows, is honoured by posterity because he was the last to discover America.
> Irresponsibility is part of the pleasure of all art; it is the part the schools cannot recognise.
> There is no heresy or no philosophy which is so abhorrent to the church as a human being.
> Come forth, Lazarus! And he came fifth and lost the job.

MUSIC

Dublin rocks. And reels and jigs. It might be world-famous for its literature, but Dublin's musical heritage is just as impressive. From mid-size theatres like Vicar Street (p103) to state-of-the-art venues like the brand new O2 (off Map p105), there are gigs of every sort virtually every night of the week.

Although Dublin isn't the natural home of trad music, there are plenty of pubs who put on scheduled and improvised 'sessions' – attended for the most part by foreign visitors who frankly appreciate the form far more than most Dubs and will relish any opportunity to toe-tap to some extraordinary virtuoso performances. Comhaltas Ceoltóirí Éireann (p132, pictured below) is the spiritual headquarters of the traditional forms – the Friday night céilidh (group Irish dance) is one of the highlights of any visit to the city.

Smithfield is home to two of the best traditional bars in the city, the Cobblestone (p125) and Hughes' Bar (p125) – if you're looking for that old-fashioned atmosphere, these are the places to go.

Want to take some music home? Pay a visit to Claddagh Records (p68), where you'll find a massive collection and friendly, knowledgeable staff who will help you discern between jigs and reels, bodhráns (Irish drums) and bouzoukis.

TOP FIVE TRADITIONAL ALBUMS
> *The Quiet Glen* (Tommy Peoples)
> *Paddy Keenan* (Paddy Keenan)
> *Compendium: The Best of Patrick Street* (Various)
> *The Chieftains 6: Bonaparte's Retreat* (The Chieftains)
> *Old Hag You Have Killed Me* (The Bothy Band)

TOP FIVE SONGS ABOUT DUBLIN
> 'Raglan Road' (Luke Kelly and the Dubliners)
> 'Old Town' (Phil Lynott)
> 'One' (U2)
> 'The Auld Triangle' (The Pogues)
> 'I Don't Like Mondays' (Boomtown Rats)

SHOPPING

British and US chains dominate the Irish high street, but there are numerous independent shops selling high-quality, locally made goods. Irish designer clothing, handmade jewellery, unusual home wares and crafts, and cheeses to die for are readily available if you know where to look. While souvenir hunters can still buy Guinness magnets and shamrock tea towels, a new breed of craft shop offers one-off or limited-edition souvenirs. Traditional Irish products, such as crystal and knitwear, remain popular and you can find modern takes on the classics.

Grafton St (Map p39) and its environs is where you'll find the city's best department stores, clothing and music chains, while immediately to the west in the warren of streets known as SoDa (Map pp80–1) you'll find specialist boutiques and funky shops. Temple Bar (Map p65) is where you'll find record shops, vintage clothes, kooky knick-knacks and markets. North of the Liffey, Henry St (Map p105, D3), just off O'Connell St, is given over to high-street chains and midrange department stores. If you're in the hunt for antiques, make your way to Francis St (Map p97, E2).

Most shops are open from 9am or 10am to 6pm Monday to Saturday (until 8pm Thursday) and from noon to 6pm Sunday. Almost all accept credit cards, and ATMs are everywhere.

TOP FIVE GUARANTEED IRISH
> Avoca Handweavers (p42)
> Barry Doyle Design Jewellers (p83)
> Cathach Books (p42)
> Louis Copeland (p111)
> Sheridan's Cheesemongers (p45)

TOP FIVE BOUTIQUES
> Chica (p43)
> Alias Tom (p41)
> Smock (p85)
> Costume (p83)
> Cleo (Map p59)

TOP FIVE MUSEUM SHOPS
> Chester Beatty Library (p79)
> Dublin Writers Museum (p107)
> Irish Museum of Modern Art (p99)
> National Gallery (p55)
> Trinity Library Shop (Map p40)

TOP FIVE DUBLIN MARKETS
> Cow's Lane Designer Mart (p68)
> Coppinger Row Market (p83)
> Moore Street Market (p111)
> George's Street Arcade (p84)
> Blackrock Market (p130)

THEATRE

Dubliners have a unique affinity with theatre; it seems to course through their veins. Perhaps this explains why dramatists Oliver Goldsmith, Oscar Wilde and George Bernard Shaw conquered the theatre world in London even before there was such an entity as Irish drama. While Dublin has a long association with the stage – the first theatre was founded here in 1637 – it wasn't until the late-19th-century Celtic Revival Movement and the establishment of the Abbey Theatre (p118) that Irish drama really took off.

After years in the doldrums following the successes of famous playwrights Wilde, Yeats, Shaw and Beckett, Irish theatre is now undergoing something of a renaissance. The Abbey has found a couple of stars in Conor McPherson and Mark O'Rowe, while the Gate (p118) does a roaring trade in high-quality productions usually starring a big name or two – don't be surprised to see a major Hollywood star treading these particular boards.

If you want something different, and there are a number of new companies staging thought-provoking, contemporary plays, you'll have to settle for smaller venues and spaces, including converted pub rooms. Look out for the likes of **Rough Magic** (www.rough-magic.com).

Theatre bookings can usually be made by quoting a credit-card number over the phone; you can collect your tickets just before the performance. Expect to pay anything between €12 and €20 for most shows, with some costing as much as €25. Most plays begin between 8pm and 8.30pm. Check out www.irishtheatreonline.com.

Relaxing in the Chester Beatty gardens below the imposing Dublin Castle (p79)

BACKGROUND

HISTORY

ORIGINS

A casual walk around the city centre doesn't reveal much of Dublin's history from before the middle of the 18th century. Besides the city's modern Irish name, Baile Átha Claith, meaning 'Town of the Hurdle Ford' – in reference to the original Celtic settlement on the Liffey's northern bank – there is absolutely no visible evidence that the Iron Age Celts ever arrived here. But they did, around 700 BC.

Even the three 12th-century behemoths of the Norman occupation – Dublin Castle, Christchurch Cathedral and St Patrick's Cathedral – which ushered in 800 years of British rule, owe more to Victorian home improvements than they do their original fittings. The story behind the famous well by the side of St Patrick's, where the saint is said to have baptised the heathen Irish into Christianity in the 5th century, is nothing more than a tale told to visitors.

GEORGIAN DUBLIN

To get a tangible sense of Dublin's history, fast-forward through the occupation, past the outbreaks of plague and the introduction of the Penal Laws prohibiting Catholics from owning or being much of anything, until the middle of the 18th century. It was then that the Protestant gentry decided that the squalid medieval burg they lived in wasn't quite the gleaming metropolis they deserved, and set about redesigning the whole place to create Georgian Dublin.

Scarcely had the scaffolding come down on the refurbishments, however, when the Act of Union in 1801 caused Dublin to lose its 'second city of the Empire' appeal and descend into a kind of ghost-town squalor.

DUBLIN'S PALE

The phrase 'beyond the pale' originated when Anglo-Norman control over Ireland was restricted to the narrow eastern coastal strip surrounding Dublin, known as the Pale. Outside this area – or Beyond the Pale – Ireland remained a wild place, and fierce Irish warriors launched regular raids on English forces from their strongholds in the Wicklow mountains.

DISASTER & INDEPENDENCE

While Dublin escaped the worst effects of the Potato Famine (1845–51) when the staple crop was blighted by disease leading to the death of at least one million people, the forced emigration of another million or so and the general collapse of Irish rural society, Dublin's streets and squares became flooded with starving rural refugees. The British government's refusal to really address the gravity of the situation fuelled rebellious instincts; while the 19th century is littered with glorious but vain attempts to strike a blow at British power, after the Famine it was only a matter of time. Following another ill-planned revolt at Easter 1916 – which laid waste to much of the city centre and resulted in the leaders' execution in the grounds of Kilmainham Gaol – the tide turned firmly in favour of full-blown independence, which was achieved after a war of sorts lasting from 1920 to 1921.

FROM FREE STATE TO CELTIC TIGER

The partition of Ireland that followed the War of Independence wasn't to everyone's liking, so a civil war quickly ensued – more bloody and savage than the war against British rule. Thereafter, Ireland settled cautiously into its new-found freedom; conservative and Catholic, it moved carefully through the 20th century until the 1960s, when the first winds of liberal thinking began to blow. Universal free secondary education was introduced and the Republic joined the European Economic Community in 1973.

Dublin's economic climate changed dramatically in the 1990s as interest rates tumbled, business burgeoned and (mostly US) foreign investment injected capital and led to hugely reduced unemployment. The

DIVIDED WE FALL

Dublin is split, physically and psychologically, by the River Liffey. Traditionally, areas north of the river have been poorer and more rundown, while the south boasts well-kept squares, expensive shops, restaurants and bars. But some Dubliners insist the real divide is east-west, with the wealthiest suburbs nearest the bay and the poorest suburbs to the west.

The 1960s and '70s saw major urban renewal and whole communities, who had spent generations in the inner city, were uprooted and rehoused in new towns such as Ballymun and Darndale. The lucrative land was then rezoned for commercial use, but some say the heart and soul of the city was broken.

now legendary Celtic Tiger economy continued unabated for 10 years.

And then it all went belly up: the global financial crisis of 2008, coupled with the puncture of the grossly over-extended construction bubble, led to the highest unemployment rate for a quarter century, the collapse and bailout of banks and the steady disappearance of many a foreign company, tempted by cheaper markets and lower wage costs in Eastern Europe and Asia.

LIFE AS A DUBLINER

More than 50% of Dubliners are under 30 and almost a quarter are teenagers – a fact that goes a long way to explaining the city's vibrant, liberal outlook. They are, by and large, a relaxed and easygoing bunch, generally more at home with informality than any kind of stuffiness. Dubliners may have known some good times in recent decades, but years of British rule fostered a healthy contempt for snobbery and it is generally money, rather than breeding, which impresses here.

Nevertheless, Dubliners aren't big on talking themselves up, preferring their actions to speak for themselves. Although not as pronounced as in rural areas, Dubliners are admirers of the peculiar art of self-deprecation, known locally as *an beál bocht a chur ort*, or 'putting on the poor mouth,' the mildly pejorative practice of making out that things are far worse than they really are in order to evoke sympathy – or the forbearance of creditors, of vital importance in the days when the majority of the Irish were at the mercy of an unforgiving landlord system.

As a result, Dubliners can readily engage in begrudgery – although it's something they'll only admit among their own and generally kept within the wider family. This is why Bono will get fiercer criticism for his goings on in his hometown than anywhere else in the world!

It'll take a keen ear and a well-honed sensibility to distinguish criticism from slagging (the Irish form of teasing), which is an art form in the city and an intrinsic element of how Dubliners relate to one another. It is commonly assumed that the mettle of friendship is proven by how well you can take a joke rather than the payment of a cheap compliment.

With 1.6 million people living in the wider Dublin area, that's a lot of teasing. Imagine the challenge for all of the recent arrivals to what was once a largely white, Roman Catholic city! Yet the assimilation of immigrants from Africa, Asia and Eastern Europe has been largely successful, and while some less enlightened minds will grumble about 'outsiders tak-

DID YOU KNOW?

> The city covers a land area of some 115 sq km.
> O'Connell Bridge is the only bridge in Europe that is as wide as it is long.
> Some 12% of workers travel more than 30km to work each day, more than double the distance travelled in 1981.
> If the whole of Ireland had a population density of Dublin it would have more than 300 million people.
> Around 9800 pints of beer are drunk each hour by Dubliners from Friday night to Monday morning.
> The average price for a house is €324,000.
> Women outnumber men in Dublin by 10,000.

ing our jobs' (a grumble that will surely get louder in the face of tougher economic times), most Dubliners agree that the city's growing multiculturalism has been of enormous benefit, giving greater weight to Dublin's declaration that it is truly one of Europe's most cosmopolitan burgs.

GOVERNMENT & POLITICS

At local level, Dublin is governed by three elected bodies: Dublin City Council supervises the city; a county council looks after Dublin County; and Dun Laoghaire–Rathdown Corporation administers the port town. The city version used to be known as Dublin Corporation (the Corpo), a name synonymous with inefficiency and incompetence, but the new incarnation is a progressive and admired local government. Each year, it elects a Lord Mayor who shifts into the Mansion House, speaks out on matters to do with the city and is lucky if half of Dublin knows his or her name by the time they have to hand back the chains.

ENVIRONMENT

Though Dublin does not suffer the severe air pollution that chokes some other European cities, it has its share of environmental concerns. Worst among them is traffic congestion, which has slowly but surely made gridlock a near-permanent reality of daylight hours throughout the city. Half-arsed efforts to redirect the flow of traffic through certain routes have seemingly made the problem worse, prompting commentators to stop commenting and just throw their hands up in despair.

It's not all bad news though: the long-awaited port tunnel, aimed at pulling most of the heavy traffic off the Liffey quays, finally opened in late 2006, and a subsequent ban on five-axle trucks along the quays has done much to improve the flow of traffic.

On the positive side, the city is blessed with many parks, gardens and squares. The plastic bag tax, where consumers are charged €0.22 per bag, has been a phenomenal success in reducing usage by 90% and gathering millions of euros for environmental projects.

Another, more controversial, scheme saw the introduction of charges for all green waste in an effort to encourage folks to recycle more and be mindful of what they dispose of – it now costs €2 for every bag they put out. This extra charge is an addition to the standard charge for regular rubbish – €91 a year for a 240l bin – that makes garbage disposal a fairly expensive proposition.

Dublin – like the rest of the country – is slowly coming around to its eco-responsibilities: a Building Energy Rating (BER) for all homes became compulsory in 2009, which is meant to encourage homeowners to take measures to increase energy efficiency, which can then be reflected in the asking price when they choose to sell.

FURTHER READING

You'll have obviously polished off Joyce's masterpieces, *Ulysses* and *Finnegans Wake,* before arriving in Dublin, but you'll be glad to know that the city's literary output extends far beyond the virtually unreadable. There are the classics: Flan O'Brien's brilliant *At Swim-Two-Birds* and *The Third Policeman;* Brendan Behan's pithy *The Quare Fellow;* and the Booker Prize–winning John Banville, who won for *The Sea* but whose sublime body of work also includes highlights such as *The Book of Evidence* and *The Untouchable*. A dip in the city's deep creative ocean will also reveal the likes of Anne Enright *(The Gathering)*, Sineád's brother Joseph O'Connor *(Star of the Sea)* and the recently arrived Claire Kilroy *(All The Names Have Been Changed)*.

Lighter reading includes the hilarious Ross O'Carroll-Kelly series, the latest of which is *We Need to Talk About Ross,* a hilarious piss-take of the mores of Dublin 4, the wealthy southern suburbs where being preten-tious and posh is, like, *toe*-tally normal. And don't forget Roddy Doyle, whose Barrytown quartet *(The Commitments, The Snapper, The Van* and *Paddy Clarke, Ha Ha Ha)* have all been made into films; he's gone serious

TOP FIVE FILMS
> *The Dead* (1987; John Huston)
> *My Left Foot* (1989; Jim Sheridan)
> *Adam & Paul* (2004; Lenny Abrahamson)
> *Inside I'm Dancing* (2004; Damien O'Donnell)
> *Once* (2007; John Carney)

of late, addressing the problems of alcoholism and abuse in novels like *The Woman Who Walked into Doors* and its sequel, *Paula Spencer*.

Finally, you just can't ignore Dublin's enormous contribution to the chick-lit genre. There's the queen herself, Maeve Binchy, author of 15 novels, the most recent of which is *Heart and Soul*. Hot on her heels is Cathy Kelly with 11 bestsellers and the new kid on the block, Cecelia Ahern, daughter of ex-taoiseach Bertie and the author of five books, including the mega-successful *PS I Love You* and, most recently, *The Girl of Tomorrow*.

FILMS & TELEVISION
Dublin has played backdrop to a host of excellent films (often standing in as another city, like West Berlin in the 1965 thriller *The Spy Who Came in from the Cold*) but has been less successful when starring as itself. Best of a questionable bunch include Neil Jordan's historical epic *Michael Collins* (1996); *Adam and Paul* (2004), Lenny Abrahamson's excellent portrayal of two junkies and their quixotic quest for a fix; Paddy Breathnach's *I Went Down* (1997) – called the Irish Pulp Fiction; John Crowley's enjoyable *Intermission* (2004); and Damien O'Donnell's *Inside I'm Dancing* (2004), a terrific piece about friendship and physical disability.

As far as TV goes, there have been a bunch of made-for-TV dramas based on the capital city, but the only perpetually running program is the RTE soap *Fair City,* set in the fictional suburb of Carrigstown. Every conceivable theme is dealt with here, from alcoholism to spousal abuse, from immigration to unemployment. It is RTE's most popular program, but it is still referred to by some as Fairly Shitty.

DIRECTORY
TRANSPORT
ARRIVAL & DEPARTURE
AIR
Located 13km north of the city centre, the **Dublin Airport** (www.dublin-airport.com) has a range of facilities including an exchange bureau, post office, a Dublin Tourism office, shops, restaurants, ATMs and pubs.

BOAT
From the UK, **Stena Line** (☎ UK 0870 570 7070, Dun Laoghaire 204 7777; www.stena line.co.uk) has a 1½-hour passenger-and-car service from Holyhead to **Dun Laoghaire** (☎ 280 1905) and a car-only ferry from Holyhead to **Dublin Port terminal** (☎ 855 2222) that takes 3½ hours.

Irish Ferries (☎ UK 0870 517 1717, Dublin 0818 300 400; www.irishferries.co.uk; Dublin Port Terminal) has ferries from Holyhead to Dublin.

TRAVEL TO/FROM THE AIRPORT

	Taxi	Airlink Express	Aircoach	Bus
Pick-up point	outside arrivals floor	outside arrivals floor	outside arrivals floor	outside arrivals floor
Drop-off point	anywhere	no 747: to O'Connell St & Busáras (Map p105, F3); no 748: to Heuston Station & Busáras	15 locations in Dublin: Gresham Hotel, corner of Trinity College & Grafton St, Merrion Sq, Leeson St & Dawson St; another goes to the International Financial Services Centre & Connolly Station before going north to Malahide	Eden Quay, near O'Connell St
Duration	to centre, 30min (50min in rush hour)	30-40min	30-120min (depending on destination & traffic)	60-90min
Cost	to centre, €25	adult/child €6/3	€7/1.50	€2.20/1
Other	supplementary charge of €1 for airport pick-up & additional charges for baggage	runs every 10-20min 5.45am-11.30pm	runs every 15min 5am-11.30pm (hourly midnight-4am)	runs every 20min from 5.30am-11.30pm
Contact	☎ 872 7272 or ☎ 677 2222	☎ 872 0000; www.dublinbus.ie	☎ 844 7118; www.aircoach.ie	☎ 872 0000; www.dublinbus.ie

GETTING AROUND

Dublin's train services (Dublin Area Rapid Transit or DART) and buses do little to ease the appalling street congestion. Getting around the centre is best done on foot or bicycle and trips further out should be timed to avoid rush hours. The LUAS light-rail service is efficient, but limited in its coverage.

In this book the nearest bus/train/light-rail route or station is noted by 🚌 / 🚊 / 🚋 symbols in each listing.

TRAVEL PASSES

Bus and LUAS passes should be bought in advance from Dublin Bus (right) or from the many ticket agents around the city (look for signs in shop windows). You can buy rail passes from any DART or suburban train station.

Adult (Bus & Rail) Short Hop Valid for unlimited one-day travel on Dublin Bus, DART, LUAS and suburban rail travel, but not Nitelink or Airlink (€10.20).

Bus/LUAS Pass Unlimited travel on both bus and LUAS (one/seven days €7/29).

Family Bus & Rail Short Hop Valid for one-day travel for a family of two adults and two children aged under 16 on all bus and rail services except for Nitelink, Airlink, ferry services and tours (€15.60).

Rambler Pass Valid for unlimited travel on all Dublin Bus and Airlink services, but not Nitelink (one/three/five days €6/13.30/20).

BUS

Dublin Bus (Map p105, D2; ☎ 873 4222; www.dublinbus.ie; 59 Upper O'Connell St; ⏱ 9am-5.30pm Mon-Fri, to 2pm Sat) has buses that are usually either blue and cream double-deckers or small, red and yellow ones called 'Imps'. They run from 6am to 11.30pm, with services less frequent on Sundays. Dublin's tourist heart is super-compact, so virtually any bus that lands in

AIR TRAVEL ALTERNATIVES

Although the vast majority of visitors will enter and exit Dublin's fair city via the airport, you can do your bit for the environment and arrive by boat – and have a bit of an adventure along the way. From Britain it's a cinch: you can buy a combined train-and-ferry ticket for a fraction of what you'll pay in airfare (yes, even in these budget airline times) or, if you're really on a budget, get a bus-and-ferry ticket – from London it won't cost you more than the price of a meal.

You can also arrive at another Irish port. Rosslare in County Wexford has ferry services from France and southwestern Britain while Larne, a short hop outside Belfast, is served from Stranraer in Scotland. Not only will you get to Dublin easily enough, but you can do some exploring on the way.

RECOMMENDED MODES OF TRANSPORT

	Around Grafton St	Georgian Dublin	Temple Bar	SoDa
Around Grafton St	n/a	walk 5min	walk 5min	walk 5min
Georgian Dublin	walk 5min	n/a	walk 10min	walk 10min
Temple Bar	walk 5min	walk 10min	n/a	walk 10min
SoDa	walk 5min	walk 10min	walk 10min	n/a
Kilmainham & the Liberties	bus 10min	bus 15min	walk 15-30min	walk 15-30min
O'Connell St	walk 10min	walk 15min	walk 10min	walk 15min
Smithfield	walk 15min	bus 15min	walk 10min	walk 20min
Phoenix Park	bus 20min	bus 20min	bus 20min	bus 25min

the city centre will put you within walking distance of some major sights, restaurants and shops. Buses heading to the centre have 'An Lár' (City Centre) on them. Fares are calculated on stages travelled, from €1.15 for up to three stages to €2.20 for up to 23. Tender exact change when boarding; if you pay too much a receipt is issued, which can be reimbursed at the Dublin Bus office.

Dublin Bus also runs Nitelink buses on 22 routes at 12.30am and 2am Monday to Saturday, with extra services every 20 minutes from 12.30am to 4.30am on Friday and Saturday. Buses depart from around the triangle of College St, Westmoreland St and D'Olier St (Map p105, D4). Journeys begin at €5.

TRAIN

Dublin Area Rapid Transit (DART; www .irishrail.ie) runs along the coast as far north as Howth and Malahide and as far south as Bray. Services depart every 10 to 20 minutes, from 6.30am to midnight, and less frequently on Sunday.

One-way tickets from central Dublin to Dun Laoghaire/Howth cost €2.20; to Bray it's €2.50.

LIGHT RAIL

Dublin's **light-rail system** (LUAS; ☎ 1800 300 604; www.luas.ie) runs one line from Sandyford north to St Stephen's Green and one line from Tallaght east via Heuston Station into Connolly Station. Trains run from 5.30am to 12.30am every 15 minutes and every five minutes during peak times, Monday to Friday, from 6.30am on Saturday and from 7am

Kilmainham & the Liberties	O'Connell St	Smithfield	Phoenix Park
bus 10min	walk 10min	walk 15min	bus 20min
bus 15min	walk 15min	bus 15min	bus 20min
walk 15-30min	walk 10min	walk 10min	bus 20min
walk 15-30min	walk 15min	walk 20min	bus 25min
n/a	LUAS 20min	LUAS 15min	LUAS 10min
LUAS 20min	n/a	LUAS 5min	LUAS 20min
LUAS 15min	LUAS 5min	n/a	LUAS 10min
LUAS 10min	LUAS 20min	LUAS 10min	n/a

to 11.30pm on Sunday. Fares range from €1.60 to €2.40 depending on your travel zones or a daily/weekly/monthly pass is available for €5.30/19.10/76 from the ticket machines, and €5/17.50/67 if bought from a designated newsagent.

BICYCLE
In September 2009, Dublin City Council launched **Dublin Bikes** (www.dublin-bikes.com), a pay-as-you-go bike scheme, similar to the Parisian Vélib system, with 450 bikes at 40 stations spread throughout the city centre. Cyclists will need to purchase a €10 Smart Card (as well as put a credit card deposit of €150) – either online or at any of the stations – before 'freeing' a bike for use, which is then free for the first 30 minutes and €0.50 for each half-hour thereafter.

TAXI
Taxis can be hailed on the street or found at ranks, Including those at O'Connell St (Map p105, D2), College Green (Map p39, C2) and N St Stephen's Green (Map p39, C4) near Grafton St.

It can be difficult to get a taxi after pubs close Thursday to Saturday. Many companies dispatch taxis by radio but run out of cars at peak times; be sure to book as early as you can. Try **City Cabs** (☎ 872 7272) or **National Radio Cabs** (☎ 677 2222).

Flag fall between 8am and 10pm is €4.10, then €1.03 for every kilometre thereafter; from 10pm to 8am (and Sundays and bank holidays) flag fall is €4.45 and €1.35 for every kilometre thereafter.

CLIMATE CHANGE & TRAVEL

Travel – especially air travel – is a significant contributor to global climate change. At Lonely Planet, we believe that all travellers have a responsibility to limit their personal impact. As a result, we have teamed with Rough Guides and other concerned industry partners to support Climate Care, which allows travellers to offset the greenhouse gases they are responsible for with contributions to energy-saving projects and other climate-friendly initiatives in the developing world. Lonely Planet offsets all staff and author travel. For more information, turn to the responsible travel pages on www.lonelyplanet.com. For details on offsetting your carbon emissions and a carbon calculator, go to www.climatecare.org.

PRACTICALITIES

BUSINESS HOURS

See inside front cover for standard opening hours.

DANGERS & ANNOYANCES

Dublin is one of Europe's safest capitals, but pickpocketing and car break-ins can be an issue. Increased immigration has stirred racial harassment. Though they're thankfully infrequent, report any serious incidents to the local police.

DISCOUNTS

Dublin Tourism's **Dublin Pass** (adult/child one day €35/19, two days €55/31, three days €65/39, six days €95/49) provides you with free entry to 27 attractions, free transfer on the Aircoach and 25 assorted discounts. It is available through the Dublin Tourism Centre (p165) and at the airport.

ELECTRICITY

Power supply is 220V 50Hz. The Republic uses three-pin rectangular-blade power plugs.

EMERGENCIES

Police, fire, ambulance (☎ 999, 112)
Rape Crisis Line (☎ 1800 778 888)

HOLIDAYS

New Year's Day 1 January
St Patrick's Day 17 March
Good Friday March/April
Easter Monday March/April
May Day 1 May
June Holiday First Monday June
August Holiday First Monday August
October Holiday Last Monday October
Christmas Day 25 December
St Stephen's Day 26 December

INTERNET

Internet cafes are dotted all over the city, and many of them are open until late. Try:
Global Internet Café (Map p105, D3; ☎ 878 0295; 8 Lower O'Connell St; ⏰ 8am-11pm Mon-Fri, from 9am Sat, from 10am Sun)

WI-FI HOT SPOTS
Many public places offer access to wi-fi networks. Try the following hotspots for free access: Chester Beatty Library (p79), Solas (p93), Market Bar (p93), Ron Black's (p50) or the Globe (p93).

Internet Exchange (Map p65, D2; ☎ 670 3000; 3 Cecilia St; ⏱ 8am-2am Mon-Fri, 10am-midnight Sat & Sun)

Most public libraries also offer an internet service, usually for little or no cost.

For the latest word on Dublin, visit:

Balcony TV (www.balconytv.com)
Dublin Tourism (www.visitdublin.com)
Dubliner Magazine (www.thedubliner.ie)
Fáilte Ireland (www.discoverireland.ie)
Ireland.com (www.ireland.com)
Irish Times (www.irishtimes.com)
Le Cool (www.lecool.com/cities/Dublin)
Lonely Planet (www.lonelyplanet.com)
Overheard In Dublin (www.overheard indublin.com)

MONEY
Ireland's currency is the euro (€), which is divided into 100 cents. Banks usually have the best exchange rates and lowest commission charges, though moneychangers often open later. Many post offices have currency exchange counters. There's a cluster of banks in College Green (Map p39, C2), opposite Trinity College, all of which offer exchange facilities.

ORGANISED TOURS
BOAT
Liffey Voyage (Map p105, D4; ☎ 473 4082; www.liffeyvoyage.ie; Bachelor's Walk; tours €14/8; ⏱ hourly from 10.30am-12.30pm & 2.15-4.15pm Mar-Nov) Take a historical cruise up and down the Liffey in the comfy, air-conditioned, all-weather *Spirit of the Docklands*.

Sea Safari (☎ 806 1626; www.seasafari.ie; Custom House Quay; tours €30/25; ⏱ from 10am, Feb-Oct) Be prepared to bang across the waves at up to 25 knots on a one-hour, adrenaline-pumping tour of Dublin Bay. Learn all about the Martello towers in Napoleonic times, how the Black Death avoided Pigeon House Harbour, and get a bird's-eye view into the gardens of Killiney Bay's glitterati.

Viking Splash Tours (Map pp80-1, A3; ☎ 707 6000; www.vikingsplashtours.com; Bull Alley St; tours €20/10; ⏱ up to 17 tours daily Feb-Nov) It's hard not to feel cheesy with a plastic Viking helmet on your head, but the punters get a real kick out of these amphibious 1¼-hour tours that end up in the Grand Canal Dock. All the while your 'craaazy' guide in Viking costume spins tales of the city.

HISTORICAL
1916 Easter Rising Walk (☎ 676 2493; www.1916rising.com; International Bar, 23 Wicklow St; tours €12/free; ⏱ 11.30am Mon-Sat, 1pm Sun Mar-Oct) A recommended two-hour tour run by graduates of Trinity College that takes in parts of Dublin that were directly involved in the Easter Rising. It leaves from the International Bar (Map p39).

Dublin Footsteps Walking Tours (☎ 496 0641; Bewley's Bldg, Grafton St; tours €10; ⌚ 10.30am Mon, Wed, Fri & Sat Jun-Sep) Departing from Bewley's on Grafton St (Map p39), these excellent two-hour tours weave Georgian, literary and architectural Dublin into a fascinating walk.

Historical Walking Tour (☎ 878 0227; www.historicalinsights.ie; Trinity College; tours €12; ⌚ 11am & 3pm May-Sep, 11am Apr & Oct, noon Fri-Sun Nov-Mar) Trinity College history graduates lead this 'seminar on the street' that explores the Potato Famine, Easter Rising, Civil War and Partition. Sights include Trinity, City Hall, Dublin Castle and Four Courts. In summer, themed tours on architecture, women in Irish history and the birth of the Irish state are also held. Tours depart from the College Green entrance (Map p39, C2).

Pat Liddy Walking Tours (☎ 831 1109; www.walkingtours.ie; Dublin Tourism Centre, St Andrew's Church, 2 Suffolk St; tours adult €6-22, child €5-20) Award-winning themed tours of the city by Dublin historian Pat Liddy, ranging from the 75-minute Dublin Experience to the two-hour Great Guinness Walk, which includes a queue-skipping tour of the Guinness Storehouse. Check the website for details of tour options and times. All tours depart from the Dublin Tourism Centre (Map p39, C2).

Sandeman's New Dublin Tour (Map p65, C3; ☎ 878 8547; www.newdublintours.com; City Hall; admission free; ⌚ 11am) A high-energy and thoroughly enjoyable three-hour walking tour of the city's greatest hits – and it's free: tip your guide only if you enjoyed the tour. Spanish language tours are also available.

HORSE & CARRIAGE
Along the north side of St Stephen's Green (Map p53, C2),

near Fusiliers' Arch, you can pick up a horse and carriage (around €45) for a trot around town. Most last half an hour, but you can negotiate with the driver for longer trips. Carriages hold four or five people.

LITERARY & MUSICAL
Dublin Literary Pub Crawl (Map p39, D3; ☎ 670 5602; www.dublinpubcrawl.com; Duke, 9 Duke St; tours €12/10; ⌚ 7.30pm Mon-Sat, noon & 7.30pm Sun Apr-Nov, 7.30pm Thu-Sun Dec-Mar) An award-winning 2½-hour walk-and-performance tour led by two actors around pubs with literary connections. There's plenty of drink taken, which makes it all the more popular; get to the Duke pub by 7pm to reserve a spot.

Dublin Musical Pub Crawl (Map p65, E2; ☎ 478 0193; www.discoverdublin.com; Oliver St John Gogarty's, 58-59 Fleet St; tours €12/10; ⌚ 7.30pm Apr-Oct, 7.30pm Thu-Sat Nov-Mar) The story of Irish traditional music and its influence on contemporary styles is explained and demonstrated by two expert musicians in a number of Temple Bar pubs. Tours meet upstairs at Oliver St John Gogarty's and take 2½ hours.

James Joyce Walking Tour (☎ 878 8547; James Joyce Cultural Centre, 35 N Great George's St; tours €10/8; ⌚ 2pm Tue, Thu & Sat) Excellent 1¼-hour walking tours of northside attractions associated with James Joyce, departing from the James Joyce Cultural Centre (Map p105).

TELEPHONE
The Ireland country code is ☎ 353, and Dublin's city code is ☎ 01.

Ireland uses the GSM 900/1800 cellular phone system, which is compatible with European and Australian, but not Japanese or North American phones. There are four Irish service providers: Vodafone (087), O2 (086), Meteor (085) and 3 (083). All have links with most international GSM providers, which allow you to roam onto a local service on arrival. You can also purchase a pay-as-you-go package with a local provider with your own mobile phone.

Local calls from a public phone cost €0.25 for three minutes. Public phones accept coins, phone cards and/or credit cards or you can reverse charges.

USEFUL PHONE NUMBERS
Directory inquiries (☎ 11811)
International directory inquiries (☎ 11818)
International operator (☎ 114)
Ireland/Great Britain operator (☎ 10)
Time (☎ 1191)
Weather (☎ 1550 123822)

TIPPING
Tipping is common, but is still not as expected (or as generous) as in the USA. If a restaurant adds a service charge (usually 10%) no tip is required. If not, most people tip 10% and round up taxi fares. For hotel porters €1 per bag is acceptable.

TOURIST INFORMATION
The main tourist authority is **Dublin Tourism** (www.visitdublin.com), with three walk-in-only city centre services. Dublin Tourism phone reservations are provided by Gulliver Info Res, a computerised service that provides up-to-date information on events, attractions and transport, as well as booking accommodation. In Ireland call ☎ 1 800 668 668; in Britain ☎ 0800 668 668 66; from the rest of the world ☎ 353 669 792 083. Branches can be found at:
Dublin Airport (arrivals hall; ☽ 8am-10pm)
Dublin Tourism Centre (Map p39, C2; ☎ 605 7700; St Andrew's Church, 2 Suffolk St; ☽ 9am-7pm Mon-Sat, 10.30am-3pm Sun Jul & Aug, 9am-5.30pm Mon-Sat Sep-Jun) The main branch of Dublin Tourism.
Dun Laoghaire (Dun Laoghaire ferry terminal; ☽ 10am-1pm & 2-6pm Mon-Sat)
O'Connell St (Map p105, D2; 14 Upper O'Connell St; ☽ 9am-5pm Mon-Sat)
Wilton Tce (Map p53, E3; ☽ 9.30am-noon & 12.30-5.15pm Mon-Fri)

TRAVELLERS WITH DISABILITIES
Dublin has been generally slow to embrace accessibility concerns, with many sights, hotels and shops located in historic buildings that have no disabled access and cannot have lifts or ramps installed because of preservation orders.

Public transport is also an issue, particularly with trains: you'll have to call ahead for an employee of **Iarnród Éireann** (Irish Rail; ☎ 703 3592; 🕑 9am-5pm Mon-Fri) to accompany you to the train and to help you off at your destination.

Dublin Bus' new fleet all have low floors and designated wheelchair spots (their older buses do not) and the LUAS is accessible.

INFORMATION & ORGANISATIONS

Fáilte Ireland's annual accommodation guide, *Be Our Guest,* is available from Fáilte Ireland's larger offices and lists places that are wheelchair accessible. Information and listings can also be obtained from **People with Disabilities in Ireland** (PwDI; ☎ 872 1744; www.pwdi.ie), **Accessible Ireland** (www.accessibleireland.com), **Access Ireland** (www.accessireland.info) or the **Citizens Information Board** (☎ 605 9000; www.citizensinformationboard.ie).

Other useful organisations:
Catholic Institute for Deaf People (☎ 830 0522; www.cidp.ie)
Cystic Fibrosis Association of Ireland (☎ 496 2433; www.cfireland.ie)
Enable Ireland (Cerebral Palsy Ireland) (☎ 872 7155; www.enableireland.ie)
Irish Wheelchair Association (☎ 818 6400; www.iwa.ie)

>INDEX

See also separate subindexes for See (p174), Shop (p175), Eat (p173), Drink (p172) and Play (p174).

A

accommodation 136-7
activities, *see individual activities*
air travel 158
All-Ireland Finals 26
ambulance 162
Archibald's Castle 131
architecture 58, 141
art galleries, *see* See *subindex*

B

B&Bs 136-7
Bank of Ireland 40
bars 139, *see also* Drink *subindex*
beer 12-13, 73, 99
bicycle travel 161
Bloomsday 25
boat tours 128, 163
boat travel 158, 159
Book of Kells 11
books 156-7, *see also* Shop *subindex*
Bulmers International Comedy Festival 26
bus travel 159-60
business hours, *see inside front cover*

C

cafes, *see* Eat *subindex*
canals 128
Casino at Marino 114

000 map pages

castles, *see* See *subindex*
cathedrals, *see* See *subindex*
cell phones 165
Celtic Tiger 153-4
Chester Beatty Library 16, 79
children, travel with 25, 140
Christ Church Cathedral 98
Christmas Dip@the Forty Foot 28
churches, *see* See *subindex*
City Hall 66
climate change 162
Clontarf 112
clubs 142, *see also* Play *subindex*
comedy, *see also* Play *subindex* festivals 26
Comhaltas Ceoltóirí Éireann 22, 132-3
Contemporary Music Centre
Convergence Festival 25
costs, *see inside front cover*
Croke Park 21, 26, 114, 144
Cultivate 66
Custom House 106
cycling 161

D

Dalkey 131
Dalkey Castle 131
dance, traditional 22
DART 160
disabilities, travellers with 165-6
Diversions 25
Douglas Hyde Gallery 40

drinking 12-13, 20, 33, 138-9, *see also* Drink *subindex*
etiquette 63
Georgian Dublin 62-3
Grafton Street & Around 50
Kilmainham & the Liberties 103
O'Connell Street & Around 116-18
Smithfield & Phoenix Park 125
SoDa 91-4
Temple Bar 73-5
Dublin Castle 79
Dublin City Gallery – Hugh Lane 106-7
Dublin Fringe Festival 26
Dublin Gay Theatre Festival 25
Dublin Horse Show 26
Dublin Theatre Festival 27
Dublin Writers Festival 25
Dublin Zoo 122
Dublinia & the Viking World 98-9
Dun Laoghaire Festival of World Cultures 26

E

economy 153-4
electricity 162
emergencies 162, *see also inside front cover*
environmental issues 155-6
events 23-8
exchange rates, *see inside front cover*

F

farmers markets, *see* Shop *subindex*
Farmleigh 122
fashion design 82
ferry travel 158, 159
festivals 23-8
film 157
    festivals 24, 27
Fitzwilliam Square 54
food 143, *see also* Eat *subindex*
    Beyond the Royal Canal 130-2
    festivals 26
    Georgian Dublin 60-2
    Grafton Street & Around 47-9
    O'Connell Street & Around 113-16
    SoDa 85-91
    Temple Bar 70-3
    vegetarian 86
Forty Foot Pool 28, 130
Four Courts 122
French Film Festival 27

G

Gaelic football 21, 26, 114, 144
galleries, *see* See *subindex*
Gallery of Photography 66-7
gardens & parks 145, *see also* See *subindex*
gay travellers 119, 146
    festivals 25
General Post Office 108
Georgian Dublin 52-63, 152, **53**
Georgian period 54
Gleeson, Sinéad 101
government 155
Government Buildings 54
Grafton Street 38-51, **39**

Grand Canal area 126-33, **127**
greyhound racing 21
Guinness Storehouse 12-13, 99

H

Hallowe'en 27
Handel, GF 66
Handel's Messiah 24
historic buildings, *see* See *subindex*
history 152-4
holidays 162
horse & carriage tours 164
horse racing 26, 28
hotels 136-7
Howth 112
hurling 21, 26, 114

I

Independence 153
internet access 162-3
internet resources 46, 137, 162-3
Ireland's Eye 112
Irish Museum of Modern Art (IMMA) 17, 99-100
itineraries 29-33

J

Jameson Dublin International Film Festival 24
Jeanie Johnston 109
Joyce, James 147
    Bloomsday 25
    Cultural Centre 108-9
    House of the Dead 100
    Museum 129-30
Junior Dublin Film Festival 27
Juthan, Arveene 76

K

Kilmainham 96-103, **97**
Kilmainham Gaol 18, 100

L

Leinster House 55
Leopardstown Races 28
lesbian travellers 146
    festivals 25
Liberties, the 96-103, **97**
Liffey Swim 26
light rail travel (LUAS) 160-1
literature 156-7
    festivals 25
live music 22, *see also* Drink, Play *subindexes*
Long Room 10-11, 40-1
LUAS 160-1

M

Malahide 112
Malahide Castle 112
Mardi Gras 25
markets, *see* Shop *subindex*
Marlay House & Park 130
Marsh, Narcissus 100
Marsh's Library 100
Merrion Square 55
microbreweries 73
mobile phones 165
money 162, 163
Monument of Light 107
Murray, Miceal 89
museums, *see* See *subindex*
music 148, *see also* Drink, Play *subindexes*
    choirs 58
    festivals 24, 26
    traditional Irish 22

N

National Gallery of Ireland 55-6
National Library 56
National Photographic Archive 67

Natural History Museum 57
nature reserves 112
Newman House 57
nightlife, *see* Drink, Play
   subindexes
North Bull Island 112
North Bull Wall 112
Number 29 57

O

O'Connell Street 104-19, **105**
Old Jameson Distillery 123
opening hours, *see inside
   front cover*
Oxegen 26

P

parks & gardens 145, *see
   also* See *subindex*
Phoenix Park 120-5, **121**
planning 33, 162
police 162
politics 155
population 154-5
Potato Famine 153
Prospect Cemetery 115
pubs 20, 33, 138-9, *see
   also* Drink *subindex*
   tours 164

R

recycling 156
restaurants, *see* Eat *subindex*
RHA Gallagher Gallery 58
Royal Canal area 114
rugby 24

S

Science Gallery 40
sea travel 158, 159

Shaw Birthplace 82
shopping 149, *see also* Shop
   subindex
   Beyond the Grand Canal
      130
   Georgian Dublin 59-60
   Grafton Street & Around
      41-7
   Kilmainham & the Liberties
      103
   O'Connell Street & Around
      109-13
   SoDa 82-5
   Temple Bar 68-70
Six Nations Championship 24
Smithfield 120-5, **121**
smoking 71
SoDa 78-95, **80-1**
sporting venues 21, 114,
   115, 133
sports 21, *see also individual
   sports*
   events 25, 26, 28
St Patrick's Cathedral 102-3
St Patrick's Festival 24
St Stephen's Green 14-15,
   58-9
statues 79, 107
Street Performance World
   Championship 26
Sunlight Chambers 67
swimming 26, 115, 130

T

Tastefest 26
taxis 161
telephone services 164-5, *see
   also inside front cover*
television 157
Temple Bar 64-77, **65**
Temple Bar Trad Festival of
   Irish Music & Culture 26

theatre 19, 150, *see also* Play
   subindex
   festivals 25, 26, 27
tipping 165
tourist information 165
tours 163-4
traditional dance & music 22
train travel (DART) 160
travel passes 159
Trinity College 10-11, 40-1

U

U2 14
Ulysses 25, 109, 147

V

vacations 162
vegetarian travellers 86
visual arts, *see* See *subindex*

W

walking tours 163-4
websites 162-3
whiskey 123
wi-fi 163
Women's Mini Marathon 25

Z

zoos 122

Y DRINK

Bars
Anseo 91
Bar with no name 91
Bia Bar 92
Dice Bar 125
Dragon 92
George 92-3
Globe 93
Grogan's Castle Lounge 93
Market Bar 93
Octagon Bar 73-4
Sackville Lounge 117

Sin É 117-18
Solas 93
Voodoo Lounge 125

Microbreweries
Dublin Brewing Company 73
Messrs Maguire 73
Porterhouse Brewing
    Company 73

Pubs
Bernard Shaw 91
Church 117
Doheny & Nesbitt's 62
Flowing Tide 116-17
Kavanagh's 115
Kehoe's 50
Long Hall 93
Mulligans 73
O'Neill's 50
Palace Bar 74-5
Ron Black's 50
Toner's 63

Trad Music Pubs
Brazen Head 103
Cobblestone 125
Hughes' Bar 125
O'Donoghue's 62-3
Oliver St John Gogarty's 74
Stag's Head 94

Wine Bars
La Cave 50

🍴 EAT
Bakeries
Bretzel Bakery 86
Queen of Tarts 72

Bistros
Bleu 47
Canal Bank Café 60

Burgers
Eddie Rocket's 49
Gourmet Burger Kitchen
    88

Cafes
Avoca Cafe 47
Cake Cafe 87
Cobalt Café & Gallery
    115
Harry's Cafe 48
Honest to Goodness 88
Larder 71
Nude 48-9
Queen of Tarts 72
Simon's Place 91
Soup Dragon 116

Chinese
Good World 87
Melody 116

Crêperies
Lemon 88

Diners
Elephant & Castle 70

Food Halls
Fallon & Byrne 87

French
Chapter One 115
Dax 60
French Paradox 131
L'Ecrivain 61
Leon 88-90
L'Gueuleton 89, 90
Restaurant Patrick Guilbaud
    61-2
Tea Room 72-3

Indonesian
Chameleon 70

Italian
Bar Italia 114
Bottega Toffoli 86
Café Bar Deli 86-7
Dunne & Crescenzi 61
La Taverna di Bacco 116
Steps of Rome 49
Unicorn 62

Japanese & Korean
Bon Ga 114
Ukiyo 91

Mediterranean
101 Talbot 113
Coppinger Row 87
Expresso Bar 130-1
Odessa 90
Seagrass 90

Middle Eastern
101 Talbot 113
Silk Road Cafe 90-1
Zaytoon 73

Modern European
Bang Café 60
Gruel 71
Mermaid Café 71-2
Thornton's 49
Town Bar & Grill 62

Modern Irish
Bentley's Oyster Bar & Grill 60
Bleu 47
Eden 70
Ely 61
Green Nineteen 88
Itsa4 131
Juniors 132
Shebeen Chic 90
Tea Room 72-3
Winding Stair 116

Nepalese
Monty's of Kathmandu 72

Pizza
Gotham Café 47

Steakhouses
Marco Pierre White
  Steakhouse & Grill 48
Shanahan's on the Green
  62

Traditional English
Bar with no name 85-6

Traditional Irish
Trocadero 49

Vegetarian
Blazing Salads 86
Café Fresh 86
Cornucopia 86
Govinda 86
Juice 86

⭐ **PLAY**
Cinemas
Cineworld 118
Irish Film Institute (IFI) 75
Screen 51

Clubs
Andrew's Lane Theatre 94
Button Factory 75
Lillies Bordello 51
Renard's 63
Rí Rá 94
Sugar Club 63
Think Tank 77
Tripod 94-5
Twisted Pepper 119

000 map pages

Comedy
Ha'penny Bridge Inn 75
International Bar 51
Laughter Lounge 118
Vicar Street 103

LGBT Entertainment
Panti Bar 119

Live Music
Ambassador Theatre 118
Button Factory 75
Comhaltas Ceoltóirí Éireann
  22, 132-3
Crawdaddy 94
JJ Smyth's 94
Mezz 75
Olympia Theatre 75-7
Sugar Club 63
Tripod 94-5
Twisted Pepper 119
Vicar Street 103
Village 95
Whelans 95

Performances
Abbey Theatre 118
Bewley's Café Theatre 50
Gaiety Theatre 50-1
Gate Theatre 118
Helix 114
National Concert Hall 63
Olympia Theatre 75-7
Project Arts Centre 77
Royal Dublin Society Concert
  Hall 133

Sporting Venues
Croke Park 21, 26, 114, 144
National Aquatic Centre
  115
Shelbourne Greyhound
  Stadium 133

👁 **SEE**
Archives
Contemporary Music Centre 66
National Photographic
  Archive 67

Castles
Archibald's Castle 131
Dalkey Castle 131
Dublin Castle 79
Malahide Castle 112

Cemeteries
Prospect Cemetery 115

Churches & Cathedrals
Christ Church Cathedral 98
Newman University Church 57
St Audoen's Protestant
  Church 102
St Begnet's Church 131
St Mary's Pro-Cathedral 109
St Michan's Church 124-5
St Patrick's Cathedral 102-3
St Stephen's Church 58
Whitefriar Street Carmelite
  Church 82

Eco Centres
Cultivate 66

Galleries
Bad Art Gallery 98
Cross Gallery 98
Douglas Hyde Gallery 40
Dublin City Gallery – Hugh
  Lane 106-7
Gallery of Photography 66-7
Irish Museum of Modern Art
  (IMMA) 17, 99-100
Kerlin Gallery 40
National Gallery of Ireland 55-6
Origin Gallery 57

Original Print Gallery 67
RHA Gallagher Gallery 58
Royal Institute of Architects of Ireland 58
Science Gallery 40
Taylor Galleries 59
Temple Bar Gallery & Studios 67-8

Libraries
Chester Beatty Library 16, 79
Contemporary Music Centre 66
Long Room 10-11, 40-1
Marsh's Library 100
National Library 56

Monuments & Statues
Justice 79
Molly Malone 107
Monument of Light 107

Museums
Chester Beatty Library 16, 79
Croke Park Experience 114
Dublin Writers Museum 107
Dublinia & the Viking World 98-9
Irish Museum of Modern Art (IMMA) 17, 99-100
Irish-Jewish Museum 54
James Joyce Cultural Centre 108-9
James Joyce House of the Dead 100
James Joyce Museum 129-30
National Museum of Ireland – Archaeology 56
National Museum of Ireland – Decorative Arts & History 122
Natural History Museum 57
Shaw Birthplace 82

Nature Reserves
Ireland's Eye 112
North Bull Island 112

Notable Buildings & Structures
Bank of Ireland 40
Casino at Marino 114
City Hall 66
Custom House 106
Farmleigh 122
Four Courts 122
General Post Office 108
Government Buildings 54
Guinness Storehouse 12-13, 99
Kilmainham Gaol 18, 100
Leinster House 55
Marlay House & Park 130
Marsh's Library 100
National Library 56
Newman House 57
North Bull Wall 112
Number 29 57
Old Jameson Distillery 123
Sunlight Chambers 67
Trinity College 10-11, 40-1

Parks, Gardens & Squares
Airfield Trust Gardens 128
Dillon Garden 128
Fitzwilliam Square 54
Garden of Remembrance 107
Herbert Park 129
Iveagh Gardens 54-5
Marlay House & Park 130
Merrion Square 55
National Botanic Gardens 115
Phoenix Park 123-4
St Stephen's Green 14-15, 58-9
Talbot Botanic Gardens 112

Sailing Ships
Jeanie Johnston 109

Zoos
Dublin Zoo 122

SHOP
Antiques
Design Associates 103
Fleury Antiques 103
H Danker 43-4
O'Sullivan Antiques 103

Arts & Crafts
DesignYard 43
Kilkenny 59

Body Products
Neu Blue Eriu 84-5

Books
Cathach Books 42-3
Forbidden Planet 68
George's Street Arcade 84
Hodges Figgis 44
Murder Ink 44
Waterstone's 46
Winding Stair 113

Charity Shops
Oxfam Home 103

Clothing & Accessories
5 Scarlet Row 68
A Store is Born 82
Alias Tom 41
Avoca Handweavers 42
BT2 42
Caru 83
Chica 43
Cleo 59
Costume 83
Cow's Lane Designer Mart 68
Design Centre 43

Dublin Woollen Mills 110
Flip 68
George's Street Arcade 84
Harlequin 84
Jenny Vander 84
Louis Copeland 111
Low Key 84
Optica 44
Penney's 113
Smock 85
Tommy Hilfiger 46
Urban Outfitters 69-70
Wild Child 85

Department Stores & Shopping Centres
Arnott's 109
Brown Thomas 42
Debenham's 109-10
Dunnes Stores 43
Jervis Centre 110-11
Powerscourt Centre 44
Stephen's Green Shopping Centre 45-6
Westbury Mall 47

Gourmet Food & Wine
Magills 44
Mitchell & Son Wine Merchants 60
Sheridans Cheesemongers 45

Home Decor
Avoca Handweavers 42
Decor 83
Design Associates 103
Haus 68-9
Retrospect 69
Urban Outfitters 69-70
Wild Child 85

Jewellery
Angles 41
Appleby 41-2
Barry Doyle Design Jewellers 83
DesignYard 43
H Danker 43-4
Rhinestones 44-5
Weir & Sons 46-7

Maps
Neptune Gallery 84

Markets
Asia Food Market 82-3
Blackrock Market 130
Coppinger Row Market 83
George's Street Arcade 84
Moore Street Market 111
People's Park Market 130
Temple Bar Farmers Market 69

Museum Shops
Dublin City Gallery – Hugh Lane Shop 110

Music
Claddagh Records 68
Walton's 85

Outdoor Gear
Great Outdoors 43

Photography
Irish Historical Picture Company 110

Toys
Early Learning Centre 110
Smyths Toys 113

000 map pages